CAN I SIT WITH YOU TOO?

More Tales From the Social Seas of the Schoolyard

SHANNON DES ROCHES ROSA and JENNIFER BYDE MYERS

Deadwood City Publishing
Redwood City, California

First edition 2008

Manufactured in the United States of America

This book is dedicated to the wild, wise, and wonderful families of SEPTAR, the Special Education PTA of Redwood City, who work so hard to promote inclusive environments for all of our children.

P.S. Grace Davis, we love you.

STORIES

~~~~~~~~~~~~~~~~~~~~~~

Cookie *by Pamela Merritt aka Shark-Fu*   1

My Longing to Belong *by Elisabeth Ellendorff*   5

Cootie Girl *by Beatrice M. Hogg*   9

An Open Apology to Kirk *by Tina Szymczak*   13

Betsy *by Dori Ben-David Johnston*   15

Summer Before Second Grade *by Gerard Sarnat*   17

Two Braids *by N. Chandani*   19

Share a Cookie *by Cheryl Caruolo, M.F.A.*   21

Immigrant Kids *by Wynn Putnam*   25

Free to Be You and Me *by Giedra Campbell*   27

French Lessons *by Dan Moreau*   31

That Old French Magic *by Katrina N. Mueller*   35

If I Had Grown Up Online: Reflections on Bullying
by Amy Looper   37

Dodging Bullet *by Laura Eleanor Holloway*   39

The Weirdest Kid in the World *by Mike Adamick*   41

Ski Bum *by Jennifer Byde Myers*   45

Instruments *by Lisa Lucke*   49

School Nurse *by Ken Putnam*   53

All God's Children *by Victoria A. Laraneta*   55

Face to Face With the Banality of Evil *by Anna Dalprato*   57

Mobil Oil Cans *by SK Knight*   61

A Special Education *by Gwendomama*   63

Love Note *by Wookie*   67

Schooltime Story *by Mariann Vlacilek*   69

Years Before I Was Allowed to See R-Rated Movies
by Shannon Des Roches Rosa   71

No-Win Scenario *by A.A. Matin*   73

The Absolute Clear-Headedness of Mrs. Rutland
by Louis E. Bourgeois   75

Treading Lightly Back to Middle School *by Alison Chino*   79

Pick Your Battles *by Madeline McEwen-Asker*   83

Will You Go Out With Me? *by Sarah Dopp*   87

Cheater, Cheater, Pumpkin-Eater *by Sabina Sood*   91

Shoes Can Buy Me Love *by Brian Greene*   95

Imagine This (A Narrative on Bullying) *by lastcrazyhorn*   99

Ella, Enchanted *by Suzanne LaFetra*   105

The Cure of Nowhere *by Amanda Jones*   109

Calling for Friends *by Kari Dahlen*   113

A Giver *by Kat Kan*   117

Un Angel Llamado Max *by Annelise Zoe Barriga*   119

Karen Morley *by Alison O'Brien*   125

Lines *by James Penha*   127

Miracle Turd *by Lea Hernandez*   131

Double Standard *by E. Hansen*   135

It Happened Several Years Ago
by Jessica of BalancingEverything   137

CONTRIBUTORS   139

ACKNOWLEDGMENTS   147

CAN I SIT WITH YOU TOO?

I confess I often see children through the eyes of an ignorant grown-up, having replaced my own childhood anxiety with the full-grown kind that comes from adult responsibilities and parenting. I see groups of children while I'm on the way to my tedious adult errands, see them playing in the park or lined up waiting, chattering among themselves. They all look so happy and carefree! Wouldn't it be great to have those idle afternoons, eating ice cream and playing kickball with your friends? You think?

HA!

And then you remember that the only reason anyone asked you to play kickball was because you had a pack of Hubba-Bubba bubble gum and bought your way in. And then later someone kicked dirt on your new shoes and you caught hell about it when you came home for dinner. So much for nostalgia.

This second volume of Can I Sit With You? that you are holding in your hands right now is a reminder of how childhood can be fraught with anxiety, with a yearning to be accepted and loved by the peers and adults in our lives. It's a voyeuristic look into the childhoods of talented writers willing to share the teeth-rattling anxiety of being told that they were not attractive enough, not smart enough, or did not have the right shoes.

Some of the stories in Can I Sit With You Too? are heart-breaking, some are hilarious, and some will make you squirm with embarrassment for the poor former child who had to endure what is now (thankfully) just a memory. What these tales have in common is a powerful message: we are all human beings, we are not alone, and many of us endure the same struggles.

Another great gift of these stories is a reminder to older children that they are not the only ones who get scared when they walk into a room of new faces. These wonderful stories will take you into the lives of people grappling with challenges as diverse as obsessive-compulsive disorder, being on the autism spectrum, dealing with burgeoning sexuality, or seeming "normal" on the outside, but being convinced something was wrong after being shunned or put down repeatedly.

I have to tell you, also, one of my favorite parts about this project: every one of these writers, editors, and artists generously gave their stories and time for free. Like the fantastic first volume of Can I Sit With You?, proceeds from this volume directly benefit the Special Education Parent Teacher Association of Redwood City, California (SEPTAR). One of SEPTAR's goals is to encourage inclusiveness for special needs children in their community and school district.

Enjoy these stories and the fascinating glimpse into the lives of people who may be different from you in some ways, but have the same need for acceptance and love. Share Can I Sit With You Too? with others (including children) in your life, and remember that we are not alone, that we all need someone to sit with.

SJ Alexander
Seattle, Washington
October 2008

Cookie

~~~~~~~~~~~~~~~~~~~~~~

Pamela Merritt, a.k.a. Shark-Fu
Kindergarten and First Grade

When I was four years old my parents moved my family to a middle class suburb in St. Louis County. When I looked around our new neighborhood I saw a sea of white faces. Our family was one of only two black families in the neighborhood. The ramifications of that didn't hit me until the first day of kindergarten when I walked into the classroom wearing a brand new pink frilly dress and white patent leather shoes, only to find myself greeted by looks of disgust and distress from my fellow students.

By the time that first day was over I had been pushed, spit at, called a monkey, and ignored by my teacher. I went home in tears and announced to my parents that there was no way in hell I was going back to that miserable place. My parents responded by telling me that there are ignorant racist people all over the world and, sadly, they teach their children to be ignorant and mean, too. The basic message was that I was going to have to learn how to cope because my parents held the value of a good education over the pain of prejudice.

My parents came of age during the 1950s and 1960s, so they were well aware of the pain of in-your-face racial prejudice. But their generation had risked their lives to get decent educations, and both of my parents felt that a few bruises or hurt feelings were par for the course for any person of color trying to get ahead. As far as they were concerned, I was learning a lesson young that I was going to have to learn eventually.

So I suffered and learned how to cope. I sat in the back of class and knew better than to try to make friends. After a particularly vicious beating in the girls' restroom, I even taught myself to hold my pee until I got home. Yeah, I was coping, but I was also miserable and terrified. And I wasn't learning much other than school survival skills, either.

All that changed the next year when Cookie transferred to my school.

Cookie was also black—a pure dark chocolate brown some people are blessed to be born with. She was solid where I was skinny, fearless where I was cautious, and she became my first friend at school. With Cookie I could conquer the world or at least conquer my phobia about the girls' restroom. She talked loud and didn't take crap from anyone and I quickly became her fan club of one. I began to laugh and play and ask questions and some of the other students began to hang out with me.

When I looked at Cookie I saw a strong black child and I began to realize that the weeks of racial taunts and physical attacks had taken something very precious from me. I realized that Cookie hadn't inspired something new in me, but that she had revived a spark that had died such a quiet death that I didn't even notice its passing.

I recall swinging on the playground next to Cookie one Friday afternoon, thinking that I was having fun and that I couldn't wait to come back to school. I couldn't wait to share my weekend news with Cookie over lunch, and gossip about the other girls or our older sisters. I remember going to the bathroom without fear of assault, my head held high as I walked past girls who used to haunt my nightmares but who now held no power over me. And I remember hugging Cookie goodbye and getting on the bus, not knowing that everything would change that weekend.

That Sunday after dinner my mother sat me down and told me that Cookie's mother had called.

Their family was moving because of a work transfer.

Cookie was moving away.

I cried as if someone had died, but my mother said that I should save my tears for a real tragedy. I was well grown before I learned the meaning of that, but at the time I thought Cookie moving away was the world's greatest tragedy.

Our parents took us out for burgers and fries but neither one of us ate. We promised to write and call and be friends forever. But then Cookie turned to me, took my hands and leaned forward and whispered in my ear.

"But it'll be okay if you don't write or call."

She pulled back and looked me directly in the eyes.

"You're going to be okay...you know that, right? Because we made a memory and that's what's really forever."

I nodded but my throat closed up and I couldn't form the right words.

Can I Sit With You Too?

"Come on, girl," Cookie said, and stood up with a smile. "Let's go play!"

And off we went to play together for what was to be the last time.

We quickly lost touch after Cookie moved away, but I thought of her often over the years. I hope she's happy and as confident as she was when we were young.

The cool thing is that Cookie was right.

She moved away but she left me with a memory and she also left me with the awareness that I am worthy of kindness, friendship, and laughter.

And that is still one of the most precious gifts of my childhood.

My Longing to Belong

~~~~~~~~~~~~~~~~~~~~~

Elisabeth Ellendorff

Kindergarten to Seventh Grade

"Tell me, are you looking forward to going to kindergarten?" asked the friendly neighbor lady as she bent down. I was standing next to my mother, clutching her hand for safety.

I had heard that question so often now. Everybody asked me. After all, I was four years old, and I was sure that beginning kindergarten next fall was going to be the biggest adventure in my life. And, like always, I looked at her and said, "Yes."

I thought about kindergarten. It was all so mind-bogglingly thrilling. They had built a brand new kindergarten in our part of Zurich, and the kids of my age group were going to be the first ones in it. Like most kids, the fact of something being *new* added to my excitement. My anticipation rose each day, as the spring of 1961 merged into early summer.

But I hadn't reckoned on the world of adults.

My father, a German physicist, was busy expanding his career. His big international Swiss company decided it would be a good idea for him to go to New York. My parents packed up our household, gathered their five children together, and before I knew what was happening, we were living in a different country, in a different culture, and immersed in a different language. So much for my plans to attend that lovely new kindergarten.

We moved to a small town on the Hudson, about two hours' drive north of New York City. I was placed in a preschool attached to the local elementary school. Here, in this new country, my brothers and I could prove that even if we had no say in what adults did with us, we were much better than those adults at learning languages. I don't honestly know how it happened. I learned English almost magically—at least, I thought so.

But then came that morning at preschool. We had been doing finger painting. When everybody finished, we sat at our tables, looking expectantly at our teacher.

Only something was wrong. The teacher had her eyes fixed on me. And she looked very angry. Apparently, my table hadn't met her standard of cleanliness, but I had no way to know that.

"Go," she said fiercely, "Get a sponge, and clean that away."

I just stared at her in confusion. Sponge? Never heard of it.

Then the teacher, who was very pretty and usually very composed—I liked her—glared at me as though she wanted to slap me. "A SPONGE!" she yelled. She must have thought I was being stubborn, maybe even rebellious.

I was bewildered. What had I done to make her so angry? I think I put my head on the table and began to cry.

"Please, Miss," said one of the other girls as she raised her hand, "Please. I don't think she understands. She's from Germany. She doesn't know what a 'sponge' is."

The teacher stared. Then she whipped around, grabbed the sponge from the sink and practically threw it at me. "THAT is a SPONGE! And now you clean that up, Madam!"

With my heart beating and my face red from humiliation, I did as she said.

Time flew, and soon preschool was a thing of the past. I now went to elementary school and spoke English as well as anyone. But, somehow, I was always "the kid from Germany." I never belonged. And I would have loved that. Oh, how I would have loved to belong!

My brothers didn't "belong" either. Though we had classmates with Italian names, and friends with French and Spanish names, somehow we stayed strangers.

Then one morning, while I was waiting for the school bus, one of my classmates became bored. She began looking for trouble. She pointed at me.

"My dad says if Lizzy is German, then she's a Nutsie," she said.

"A Nutsie?" the other kids giggled.

"Yeah, a Nutsie, Nutsie, Nutsie."

They put me in their middle and began dancing around me, sticking out their tongues and singing, "Nutsie, Nutsie, Nutsie!"

The bus stopped to pick us up and they broke off their singing. I was more confused than sad. A Nutsie. A Nutsy? I said the word over and over in my mind. What could they mean?

Can I Sit With You Too?

Curious, I asked my mother after school, "Mummy, what is a Nutsie? The other kids said I was a Nutsie."

My mother frowned. Then she knelt down and looked into my eyes.

"Listen. Nazis were bad people who did very nasty things in Germany. That was during the war. That was before you were born. You can't be a Nazi. I was never a Nazi, nor was your father. Your grandparents were very pious Christians. They got into very dangerous situations for not belonging to the Nazi Party."

For not belonging! For someone like me, who fiercely wanted to "belong," this was a new concept. My parents and my grandparents obviously were proud of "not having belonged" in those days.

Seven years passed, and my father was offered a professorship at a German university. So my parents packed up again and moved us back to Germany. They were glad to go. My brothers were almost finished with school now, and it was the time of the Vietnam War. Although we were officially "just residents," they, like any American boys, could be drafted.

Once again, we children were not asked about the move; the adults decided for us. With heavy hearts we said goodbye to our teachers, friends, and neighbors. I never really had succeeded in belonging, I never was invited to the really cool parties and social events, but I did have one or two dear friends I knew I would miss.

But, no matter, we were going back home now. We were Germans, and for the first time in my life, I would be living in "my" country. That would make up for a lot of sadness. Now I would belong.

So I thought.

I adapted to the so very different German school system. I gained new friends. I got used to speaking German, rather than English.

Then one day, one of my new girlfriends said to me, "Do you know what everyone calls you? How the kids who don't know your name refer to you?"

I shook my head. "No. Tell me."

"They call you 'The American Girl.'"

Cootie Girl

~~~~~~~~~~~~~~~~~~~~~~

By Beatrice M. Hogg

Age five to age eleven

When I was in grade school, I had the cooties. No one ever explained to me what "cooties" were, or how I caught them. Unlike the measles, they lasted all six years of elementary school, following me through three schools.

Over the years, I have been able to determine a few things about cooties. Apparently, only girls got cooties. Girls who developed cooties were different in some way—they were plain-looking, overweight, dressed funny, or had a strange family. Unfortunately, I fit into all of those categories.

I grew up in a small coal-mining town in western Pennsylvania called Hills Station. I was adopted when I was three weeks old, and brought to Hills from North Carolina. My adoptive parents were in their late fifties/early sixties when they adopted me, a generation older than the parents of my peers. I grew up an only child in a town of mostly large Catholic and Baptist families. When I was around four, my father retired from the mine and bought his first Cadillac, staying with that brand for the rest of his life. Only one other father in town drove a Cadillac. I was embarrassed to be seen in that car.

And there were my personal cootie credentials.

I was left-handed, so when I used pencils, I smeared the page as I wrote, leaving a gray smudge on one side of my left hand. My right-handed parents tried to teach me to tie my shoes, but by following their example I learned to tie backwards. The laces always came apart, and other kids laughed as I struggled to make my strange-looking bows.

Maybe my left-handedness also caused me to be uncoordinated. I could not hit a ball, kick a ball, throw a ball, or run. Gym class was my personal hell.

I was also smart. All of the black kids accused me of trying to be white because I did well on tests.

I was chubby and dark-skinned, with short nappy hair and big feet. I got a new outfit for the first day of school and new dresses for Christmas and Easter, but that was it. Most of my clothes were ill-fitting hand-me-downs from my neighbor, Holly, who was older and bigger than me.

Six years of cootie-ness. I started first grade at five, because of some law related to my birth month and the fact we had no kindergarten. I was a year younger than most of my classmates. My first school was Hills School, a two-room schoolhouse across the street from my house. During my first week of school, I fell when the recess bell rang and was trampled by the other kids. I still have a scar on my leg from the rock that was embedded in my knee that day. In gym class, no one wanted me on their team. No one wanted to drink from the water fountain after me, as cooties were contagious. Since my last name was Hogg, every morning's roll call was punctuated by oinks and snorts.

For fourth grade, I had to go to Canonsburg, the nearest big town. By then, a new elementary school was being built outside of Hills. But until it was finished, I had to catch a bus every morning to First Ward School. Riding the bus was stressful. If I was first in line, I got a seat all to myself, as no one wanted to sit next to me. If had to share a seat, the other kid tried to move as far away from me as possible, so no cooties could jump on them. The boys in the back of the bus made jokes. One of the worse insults imaginable was, "You like Marvella Hogg." Everyone on the bus would laugh, as no one could imagine someone liking me. I pretended not to hear.

One month after the start of my fifth year of school, Hills Hendersonville Elementary School opened. I no longer had to ride the bus, but now my father drove me to school in the dreaded Cadillac. Kids snickered as I got out of the car, either because of the car or because of my gray-haired father.

At ten, I wore the same shoe size as my mother, seven and a half. My mother thought that a sturdy, brown brogan would be the best shoe for school. The big, heavy shoes made me look like a cartoon character.

In fifth and sixth grade, I hated test days. Kids sitting near me would try to copy my papers. I had to be a contortionist, trying to cover my work while answering the next question.

Even my cousin and girls I grew up with made jokes about me behind my back. At Hills-Hendersonville, we had a cafeteria. Neither the black kids nor the white kids wanted me to sit with them, so I sat at the end of a table by myself. Finally, the two years of torture were over, and I was in junior high.

I wish I could say that Cecil Junior High was better, but it was more of the same. I started wearing glasses at twelve, and my mother died the summer after seventh grade, when I was thirteen. And don't get me started about puberty. But I survived.

I am now over fifty and I still don't fit in. But what was once weird is now just eccentric. I have friends who are unique, too, and I don't ever have to kick a ball if I don't want to. I shop at thrift stores, buying the discarded clothes of strangers, but I get to pick them. And now, I like my unusual name. Growing up as a Cootie Girl has made me more sensitive, a quality I use in my writing. They may have been laughing at me then, but as a writer, I can have the last word—in print. Cootie Girls Rule! (Stick tongue out here.)

An Open Apology to Kirk

~~~~~~~~~~~~~~~~~~~~~~

Tina Szymczak

Age six at the time

Dear Kirk,

I am sorry that I did not stick up for you more in the first grade.
I am sorry that I didn't ask you to come to my house to play.
I am sorry that you didn't get to live with a forever family.
I am sorry that the kids at school were so horrible to you.
I am sorry that they called you "Kirk the Jerk."
I am sorry that I do not remember your last name.

If I could do it all over,

I would have played with you at recess when no one would, *every* day, not just sometimes.

I wouldn't have let go of your hand when we were walking home and other kids were coming.

I would have shared my Jos Louis with you on the field trip and sat with you on the bus.

I would have been your best friend.

I am glad that I kicked those boys *hard* with my Cougar boots that day they were bullying you after school. I wish that there wouldn't have been a need for anyone to have to protect you. I wish people would have been nice to you and that grown ups would have made the world a safer place for you.

I think of you often. I feel much shame and sadness for the things that never were and all that should not have been. When I watch my son as he struggles so much to fit in, I often think of you. I will do better by him than what was done for you.

I am sorry and I hope life got better. I hope you found someone to sit with on the bus, someone who would share their lunch with you.

Can I Sit With You Too?

Betsy

~~~~~~~~~~~~~~~~~~~~~~

Dori Ben-David Johnston

Age six at the time

Betsy was small and frail. She barely had eyelashes. Her hair was thin and wispy, and in my memory, it was silvery-gray although I don't know if it really was. She had a weak voice, high-pitched and a little whiny. She also had a skin condition. Maybe it was eczema, maybe something more serious. But her skin was very dry and easily irritated. White, flaking pieces dotted her body—her arms, her legs, her face. Her hands were dry and wrinkly. She looked like a little old lady in a child's body. She wasn't supposed to wash with soap, or even too often with water.

Our torment of her was relentless.

We were six years old, Betsy and I and most of our first grade class. A few times each day, the class would line up in the hallway outside the restroom. Six at a time, we would go in, use the restroom and wash our hands. It was usually one of these bathroom breaks that triggered the torment—we called her gross, said she was dirty, said how nasty it was that she didn't wash her hands with soap and water. She would protest and plead in her small, thin voice, "But I'm not supposed to use soap!"

I don't actually remember if I ever said anything myself. My only memory is of us standing in a circle, surrounding Betsy, tormenting. And of her protesting, defending.

Every afternoon we were released for recess. Together the class walked across the huge grassy lawn towards the playground. Once we crossed an invisible threshold, we all took off running. One day I lingered behind and was one of the last to reach the playground. As I darted up a ladder, my teacher called my name—and immediately I was filled with dread. I knew what was coming: "Today you play with Betsy." Great, just great. I slowly turned around and trudged disappointedly towards Betsy.

My Dad taught at my school so I stayed late every day, waiting for him to take me home. I would hang out in the front lobby, moving from couch to couch and chatting with the receptionist, Paula, who always had a piece of gum for me.

I was hanging around the lobby one afternoon when I heard Betsy's high voice. It had a different tone than I was used to hearing from her—she sounded happy. I heard her excitedly yell, "Daddy!" as a man came down the hall towards her with his arms spread wide. She ran to him with a huge smile, and jumped into his arms. He hugged her and spun her around.

I was bewildered. This guy clearly loved Betsy. Betsy, with the weird skin who didn't use soap when she washed her hands.

Betsy went to a different school after first grade, and I didn't think about her for almost twenty years. Then she popped back into my mind one day. I'm not sure what made me think of Betsy—maybe it was having children of my own and thinking about their vulnerability.

Now I think about Betsy all the time. I hope she's happy.

Can I Sit With You Too?

Summer Before Second Grade

~~~~~~~~~~~~~~~~~~~~

Gerard Sarnat

Age six at the time

Outside home, digging rich loam coated with city block soot,
I notice a carrot-topped freckly face
against the inky flaming sunset.

Auburn, fair, and more than a bit stippled myself;
fingernails chock full of dirt;
uncertain why; I leave the boys to move my bones closer.

At first I circle in, pursuing nearer and nearer until I just
plop down beside the new girl.

Never before thusly stirred to thrust my body,
the world mocking me, a bushel of apples
crushing a soft tomato.

Still—eventually gathering steely courage,
not sure what I'm doing—before I know it, I lean over
and at the tender age of six, cannot resist the bliss,
plant my first non-family kiss in our neighborly wading pool.

Two Braids

~~~~~~~~~~~~~~~~~~~~

N. Chandani

Elementary School

My parents came to the United States in the hope of achieving prosperity. They were both doctors. They met each other in New York and, shortly afterwards, got married.

While growing up in India, my mom always had long, thick black hair in two braids like Pippi Longstocking. She put my hair in the same two braids for school in the United States.

I remember my first years of grade school with vivid horror. It was difficult enough to have a different name than everyone else, let alone be the only girl in first grade to have long, thick black hair and two braids attached to my head. Let's just say Pocahontas was my newly established nickname.

All the other first grade girls had simple names like Sarah and Julie. They had short blonde hair with cute barrettes and ribbons. I pondered time after time why my mother couldn't see this. Was she blind? At that time I didn't want to be Indian, I just wanted to be a "normal" first grader.

Every day I would beg my mom, to please let me have one braid. I would have eaten my vegetables, done my homework, done *anything* to get rid of the dreaded two braids. But, no. Every day my mom would put my hair in those two ugly braids, and off to school I would go.

But I had a trick up my sleeve: as soon as I got on the big yellow bus to go to school, I would wrap one braid around the other, to give the illusion of one braid. It was pathetic, I know, but I desperately wanted to fit in.

I particularly remember school picture day. My mom, as usual, put two braids in my hair and even got a little fancy with pink sparkly barrettes and a little bit of rouge on my cheeks. When I got on the bus, I got the courage to take the braids out completely. Finally, for the first time, I felt like everyone else! I took my first grade pictures confidently, with my hair free and flowing.

My mom received my school pictures a couple of months later. She didn't say much, but her look of hurt and disappointment is one I will never forget. A look of pain that only a mother could have. At the time I did not realize what the big deal was. I thought my mother's goal in life was to make me miserable. Why would it matter if my hair was in braids or just loose?

I am twenty-one now, and just recently I believe I understand why my two braids meant so much to my mother. The braids themselves were meaningless, but their symbolism was everything. In my mother's eyes, I was denying her culture every time I asked her to take out my braids. She felt as though I was embarrassed of her, of where we came from. My mother knew that over time I would lose certain parts of my culture, but she didn't realize it would begin so early. Perhaps this is why she held on to the braids. She wanted me to have a piece of who she was. She never again asked to put the braids in my hair, and to be honest I was not about to ask her to do so.

Today, I still have a tough time looking at myself as the world truly sees me. When I look at myself, I see me as I see everyone else around me; sometimes I forget that I am Indian even though no matter what I do I can't deny it. Freeing myself from Pippi Longstocking and Pocahontas won't help me run away from who I am. I will always be the little girl with long black hair and two braids, with the name no one can pronounce, the name that stands out. I will never be the girl with blonde hair and blue eyes. I will never have the family who drinks milk with their dinner.

And I am happy with that. Even if I don't look, act, or sound like everyone else, that's okay. There comes a point in each of our lives where we can either use our differences as an advantage, or be inhibited by those differences.

Never let adversity define your life.

Share a Cookie

~~~~~~~~~~~~~~~~~~~~

Cheryl Caruolo, M.F.A.

Age seven at the time

Because my parents never made much of an effort to create opportunities for me to be with other children, I had no idea how to share or play games when I entered school. Mom was overprotective and never allowed me to participate in after-school games or activities like Girl Scouts. She was afraid of everything. And I followed suit.

In 1966, my uncle took us to visit the World's Fair in New York City. The Fair was filled with electric cars of the future, street performers from Europe and Latin America, and a roller coaster that careened through the middle of a building. But Mom wouldn't allow me to go inside any of the attractions or on any of the rides. My uncle finally convinced her to go on the skyline so we could see the whole fair from above, but my mother was so scared I'd fall out that she held a tight grip on the collar of my coat, the whole time. I wasn't tall enough to see over the edge of the car, so I never saw that view of endless possibilities.

Once my class went on a field trip and I was left behind because my mother didn't give me permission to go. Since anything unfamiliar terrified me, when my teacher told me to go to the classroom next door, I panicked and started to cry. My classmates laughed. I cried more. I told my teacher that I wanted to stay in our classroom.

"You can't stay here alone."

"I'm not alone. The angels are here with me."

They laughed harder.

My teacher warned the class to stop and then, in a perfect single line, they left. I remember feeling relieved, thinking I could stay right in my familiar seat until the end of the day. But a few minutes later another teacher came into the room to get me.

"Come along now to my classroom."

At seven years old my choices were limited, and so with red eyes and a runny nose I followed her into her room.

When I arrived at the schoolyard the next day, the snickers of my classmates surprised me like a splash of cold water.

"Cry baby."

"No one has imaginary friends anymore."

I dreaded recess. Usually no one would play with me, so I sat in the corner of the schoolyard, rolling stones under the shadow of an oak tree. The tree's umbrella felt safe. Sometimes I'd look through the little steel windows of the fence and wish I was in a Mustang convertible or Corvette Stingray speeding down the main road. I'd watch the girls on the asphalt playing hopscotch—a game I was good at—but never had the nerve to join them.

Whenever the class was asked to choose team members, I always ended up assigned to a team as a leftover. If I was lucky enough to be one of the first ones out the door at recess, I'd run to the end swing and stay on it for the entire time. I loved gliding back and forth through the air, looking up at the sky. Pretending to fly. The higher, the freer.

I remember telling my mother that I hated school, but I never explained why. I didn't want to admit that none of the children liked me. I understand a parent wanting to protect her young, but Mom's fears stunted me from developing self-confidence—I struggle with it still, today.

In second grade I tried to start anew. I stopped talking about imaginary friends and pretended to like all the things my classmates liked. But things fell apart quickly.

Unable to participate in after-school activities and forbidden to invite friends home, my life grew more isolated. I pulled deeper into myself like a turtle retreating into its shell. The unresolved feelings that hung in the air resulted in bouts of anger, depression, and confusion. Once I picked a fight with a girl simply because I knew I could beat her up. I derived great satisfaction from that poor girl's agony. My young life was out of control and I desperately wanted control over something.

My life drudged on until I was finally able to convince my parents to let me get a dog—a six-month-old Wiemaraner. Because she was German and I was nine, I named her Heidi. Suddenly, I had a companion. I adored that dog.

Heidi woke me every morning for school and was waiting every afternoon when I returned. Sitting on the porch together, I'd scratch her ears as she rested her head on my lap. Her gray hair felt like short slips of satin sliding through my fingers.

Can I Sit With You Too?

I felt unconditional love and acceptance from Heidi. We were connected in that unspoken spiritual way humans and animals seem to share. Whenever I was crying she'd place her paw on my hand and nuzzle her head alongside mine. If anyone was visiting our house and she was unsure of them, she would sit in between us until I'd assure her that everything was okay.

Because of Heidi, I started to believe in myself the tiniest bit. And I gradually felt more comfortable talking to kids at school—finding things in common, sharing snacks, even sometimes joining hopscotch games.

Then one day a new girl came to class. My classmates pointed at her and called her weird. I said nothing. But at recess one brilliant blue autumn day, I noticed her swaying on my safe-haven swing and, for some unexplainable reason, I walked up to her and offered her one of my beloved Oreo cookies.

Can I Sit With You Too?

Immigrant Kids

~~~~~~~~~~~~~~~~~~~~~~

Wynn Putnam

Age seven at the time

When I was almost eight years old, my family emigrated from Holland to Ontario, Canada. Because we spoke only Dutch, our new teacher put me, my twin sister, and my two older sisters all in grade one. They said that once we learned to speak English, they would reevaluate us to see if my twin and I should really be in grade three, and my older sisters in grades four and six.

We were in a one-room schoolhouse, so we felt awkward and big sitting in the grade one row while kids our own size sat on the other side of the room, at the back. When the older, bigger kids would point and snicker at us we did not know what they were saying so we smiled at them. We wanted to learn to speak English, join in with their fun, and sit with them.

This was a country schoolhouse, so everyone brought their lunch. At noon we followed the other Grade Ones, got our lunch bags from the hall, and started to eat. But one day when we went to get our lunch bags, a couple of the bigger kids went in front of us and grabbed them. They looked in our bags, ate what they liked, then tossed the bags into the garbage.

My sister and I went back to the classroom and tried to communicate to the teacher that these kids had taken our lunch. We could not say what had happened, and she thought that we did not have a lunch that day. Apparently a kid at the back said that we had already eaten our lunch and some other kids laughed. We started to point at the kids who had taken our lunch and made gestures with our hands, when the teacher took an apple out of her own bag and started to cut it in half. We shook our heads and started to cry.

Suddenly, a few of the younger children came over to our desk and gave us some of their lunch. I can't remember exactly what, a cookie or an orange, but they wanted to share. We stopped crying, smiled, and told each other in Dutch that the foods we were now being given were delicious, even better than what had been in our lunch bag. We communicated our thanks to these kids by smiling and making gestures of what we were trying to say.

For a while we put our lunch bags in our desks, because it took quite a bit more time before we could speak English well enough to tattle on the few kids who tormented us because we spoke a different language. Most kids in the class tried to help us belong, even when they could see how big we looked in the grade one row, and heard us talking in a strange language.

Smiling faces are the same in every language, and it's easy to communicate with other kids that way and join in their fun. Kids like to sit with you when your face shows a friendly smile. Even if you cannot speak their language, they understand.

Free to Be You and Me

~~~~~~~~~~~~~~~~~~~~~~

Giedra Campbell

Age eight to present

In fourth grade I started going to a small magnet school. That first year it was easy to be friends with all the girls in my class—there were only seven of us, and eighteen boys. We seven hung fairly closely together, in part because of the efforts of Ms. Shainey, our teacher, who arranged special activities with the girls so we wouldn't be overwhelmed by all those boys. She told us that women could be anything they wanted, and used us to help teach diversity workshops. She'd have us act out scenes from a record called Free to Be You and Me to teach about prejudice and stereotypes. In my scene, my friend Amanda and I pretended to be babies, and to be confused about who was a girl and who was a boy ("You're bald, so you must be a boy"). Our scene showed how you shouldn't make assumptions about someone based on looks, nor limit someone based on their sex.

Come fifth grade, the number of girls in the class rocketed up to fourteen, and that's when cliques started forming. Two of the new girls and five of the fourth grade group formed a group they called the Super Seven. I don't know that they ever actively shunned me, but for whatever reason, I was not part of their group. They gathered on the parallel bars, separate and superior. Meanwhile over at the jungle gym, four of the new girls and I became the Fabulous Five. We modeled the name on the Super Seven, but we didn't really know what our club was supposed to do.

Probably the Super Seven didn't know either, but it seemed like the Super Seven was about boys and clothes. Those girls were the ones who were "going with" boys (and kissing! on the obstacle course!) or at least excited about the possibility. We Fabulous Five were uncomfortable with that idea. The only thing I remember from our club was talking about how horrendous it would be to get your period, and to therefore have to carry a purse. We'd then scan the playground looking for purses so we could gossip about their owners, even as we'd just admitted that such attention would be awful.

There were three other girls in the class, too. I am embarrassed to confess that we called them the Terrible Three. Not only is it not alliterative, but I can't think of a single terrible thing about them. They just happened to be the most different. Valentina, who had been in fourth grade with the rest of us, was the youngest in the class by over a year and had the longest hair in school. Shaleena was the only black girl in the whole program, and had a British accent. And she wore a bra. Because she needed to. And she carried a purse. And the last girl, Phillipa, well, I can't even identify a difference in her case. She was the tallest girl in the class, but were we really that shallow? (In hindsight I see that all three also had unusual names, but by that criterion, clearly I should have been in their group!)

The groups did not stay the same for long—I don't even remember how long those "clubs" lasted, but certainly there was shuffling of alliances all throughout sixth grade and junior high. By the time we got to high school, my best friends were Kara, a fellow Fabulous Fiver, and Shelley and Amanda—two of the Super Sevens. Throughout junior high we cemented our friendships mostly through our time in choir and drama together, making up silly dances for talent shows and musicals, and skipping through the halls of our junior high singing "Follow the Yellow Brick Road" and "Born Free!" at the top of our lungs.

In ninth grade, we made new friends, but also stayed close to one another. Or so I thought. Until I read what Amanda wrote in my yearbook:

> "…I'm glad that us four got to be good friends last year and this year. But understand that I changed a lot, and by the end of the summer I'll need some constant and reliable friends. I just don't like singing in the hallway and dancing. I dunno, it's fun at someone's house but otherwise it's embarrassing—pretty soon it'll hit you and you'll die! Sorry—this sounds so degrading, but the truth is you're such good friends. Anyway, loosen up and learn to party…"

And just like that, Amanda and I were never friends again. I don't think she meant to hurt my feelings; she was only being honest. Though

Can I Sit With You Too?

the words stung, she couldn't help it that the goofy antics of a big ole drama geek made her uncomfortable. But her discomfort with me was no different from the discomfort I felt about her world of popular kids. I know I felt just as negatively about her group as she felt about mine.

By the end of high school, Shelley and Valentina were among my closest friends—never mind our having been in three separate cliques in fifth grade. The glue that held us together was in fact our shared experiences since fourth grade, and of course the fact that we all still thought singing in public was amusing.

As for Amanda? She died in a car accident, less than a month after we graduated. I was traveling at the time. When I returned home, my mother gave me a newspaper containing the story, and I sat on the floor in my room reading it over and over again. The article described how Amanda had come in from riding her skateboard, had donned something for going out, and had parted from her dad for the last time, saying in her hip way, "Later days, Dad." (The article's next line? "There would be none.") The article spoke of the career in architecture that was not to be, and of Amanda's many, many friends. They made her sound so full of potential, so bright, so friendly, so loved.

I had mixed feelings. I didn't know how to mourn someone who was apparently too cool for me, even if she had once been a friend.

Twenty years later, I believe that Amanda was all of the things the article said she was. Of course she probably would have changed her major and career when she got to college, but she probably was a wonderful friend to her friends at the time, and she had a promising future. And I also believe that she would have matured out of the cliquish high school place that led her to drop me as a friend—and even to tell me so in writing!

Nowadays, I have friends who were part of the popular crowd at their high school—people I know I would have avoided at the time. I bet Amanda would by now have made friends with some drama people. These days, she might have even been okay with watching me stand in public somewhere and belt out "...and you and me are free to be, you and me." I'd like to think so, anyway, because if no one appreciates differences, then there really is no point to being free to be *you* and to be *me*.

French Lessons

~~~~~~~~~~~~~~~~~~~~

Dan Moreau

Age eight at the time

When I was eight, my family moved from Miami, Florida to Bangkok, Thailand, and my parents enrolled me in the French School. Unlike the American School, which cost more and was farther from our house, the French School embodied my mother's ideals of sophistication, culture and civility. (She had been raised by French Catholic nuns, but instead of rebelling against them as other girls did, she embraced them.)

I had just finished first grade in Miami, but because I was starting at the French School with no preexisting knowledge of French, the principal thought I should repeat the first grade. My parents didn't object, nor did I.

One early September day, my parents dropped me off by the front gate of my new school and wished me luck. Somehow I managed to find my classroom. Our teacher's name was Madame Unarat. She was petite and plump with short dark hair and owlish glasses. That first morning I sat quietly at my desk, pretending to understand everything that my new classmates and teacher said.

At noon, the bell rang for lunch, and Madame Unarat let us out into the courtyard. All the other kids had brought packed lunches. Everyone except me. I think my parents had sent me off to school without lunch, assuming—and perhaps rightly so—that the expensive tuition they were paying would at least include meals. It didn't.

As I sat by myself on a bench, biting my fingernails, my stomach growling, a woman who worked at the school approached me. She was wearing lipstick and perfume and the collar of her blouse was stylishly raised up. She asked me if I had eaten. I didn't say anything. She repeated herself, this time in English. I shook my head in reply.

She took me to the school cafeteria. They called it a "cafeteria," but it was more like a French bistro with a chalkboard out front that displayed the day's specials. It was where the teachers and school staff gathered for lunch, coffee, and cigarettes. The woman bought me a chicken drumstick and took me back to the courtyard, where I devoured the drumstick down to the bone.

A boy from my class sat next to me on the bench. He was the biggest kid in our class and looked older than the rest of us, with the lip shadow of a prepubescent mustache. He spoke some English and, unlike the other kids, who as a rule ignored me, he was friendly to me. Too friendly. But where he was talkative and warm, I was aloof and tightlipped.

Though it was only my first day and I didn't understand a word of French, I instinctively knew where this boy stood in the playground hierarchy. In approaching me so early on, he might have befriended me before I caught on to what the other kids were saying about him. But I made a swift and vital decision. I would rather have no friends at all than be associated with a social pariah.

Slowly but surely, as my French improved, so did my rapport with my classmates. I made new friends; he didn't. We never talked much after that.

Because of my age and because of the mistaken belief that children pick up languages like head lice—by proximity and by immersion—my parents thought I would come home one day, fully fluent in French. That wasn't the case. I had to learn French like any adult would, through repetition, rote memorization, and trial and error.

Every day after school I met with Madame Unarat for an hour or two. That was where my true instruction took place. Her methods were simple yet effective. She would read from a primer, pausing after each word, which I repeated until she was satisfied with my pronunciation. It was painstaking, frustrating, and laborious, and sometimes she would raise her voice in anger when I couldn't sound out a word correctly. But it worked. By the end of the year, I spoke enough French to get by, and was admitted to the second grade.

My second grade teacher, Monsieur Stricte, was a dark, wiry, morose man. He didn't have Madame Unarat's patience and treated me like any other student. By then, I had quit having afternoon lessons with Madame Unarat. It was assumed that I was fluent.

I wasn't. I spoke a hybrid of playground argot and slang. Yet I went to great lengths to conceal my failings. I copied off of classmates, I cheated on reading comprehensions by looking up the answers in the back of the book and, most of all, I kept a low profile. To my parents and everyone else, I seemed to be doing just fine.

One day, in the middle of the semester, Monsieur Stricte asked me point-blank if I spoke French. I had just handed in an assignment on which I had done better than everyone in the class. Like with every other assignment, I had cheated on this one, but my mistake was to give myself too many correct answers.

Monsieur Stricte stared at me coldly. His eyes said it all. I knew the answer he was looking for. To say "yes" would perpetuate a charade he plainly saw through. It would also be a lie. Yet the truth was more complicated. Yes, I spoke conversational French. But my written French and reading skills were awful. After a few awkward seconds, I shook my head.

The following day, I was demoted to the first grade, where Madame Unarat welcomed me, literally, with open arms, wrapping me up in a tight bear hug in front of the entire class. I had never been so happy to see her.

Can I Sit With You Too?

That Old French Magic

~~~~~~~~~~~~~~~~~~~~~

Katrina N. Mueller

Third Grade

It all started with a cloud.

Stacy was proud of her French heritage and would flaunt it at every opportunity. She was tall and thin, with long, straight hair down to her bottom. My small, chubby body and mop of unruly curls seemed ugly by comparison. I was in awe of her. Stacy was exotic and beautiful and strong, like a fantastical bird of prey. I felt lucky, and a little confused, whenever she acknowledged my existence.

One day, in early March, Stacy and I were playing on the swings. We were chattering idly when suddenly she glanced up and gave a startled shriek. I jumped and looked around wildly for the cause of her alarm.

"Stacy! What's wrong?"

She let her swing slow and then stop, pausing dramatically before she pointed into the sky with a trembling finger. "It's him," she gasped. "It's the Snake!"

The proper noun status of the word was apparent in her voice. I followed the line from her finger to a single, thin cloud in the sky. It looked vaguely like a kite, or a snake, I supposed. It was a rough diamond shape with a trailing wisp behind it. Curiosity overwhelmed my fear and I said timidly, "…the Snake?"

Her deep brown eyes were wide as she imparted the tale:

"Several generations ago, my family was cursed by Gypsies. No one is allowed to speak of what happened, but ever since that day, the Snake has been following us. It watches from above, waiting, following us and using its dark French magic against us. It's…oh no!" She cried out again and stared at the snake. "It's *déjà vu*!"

"What is *déjà vu*?" I said, as panic gripped me. If there was any sort of strange French magic going on, I wanted no part of it! "Stacy! What is *déjà vu*?"

She looked at me again and whispered, "*Déjà vu*...It's an old French magic." I leaned close, afraid to hear more but too enthralled to stop her. "It's like going back in time. The Snake is sending me back in time! I'm having *déjà vu*, and you're a part of it...I remember sitting on the swings with a girl like you. A blond girl in a purple coat! You're a part of my *déjà vu*!"

I stared at the Snake in the sky, paralyzed. The shape of the cloud had sagged and melted, but it didn't matter. The Snake had already cast its magic on me. I had gone *déjà vu* with Stacy. My life, I realized, wasn't my own. I was part of Stacy's *déjà vu*. I didn't exist, except as a part of the Snake's dark magic.

I don't exist! And at that thought, my uncertain grip on reality shattered. I ran blindly, screaming, from that thought. Only later did I realize I could hear her laughing as I ran.

I'm not sure how long I was lost in that frenzied state. I remember being sent home from school because I kept babbling about not existing—deep thoughts for a third grader! It took a while for me to realize I still existed apart from Stacy's monster snake-in-the-sky.

To this day, I still shudder helplessly when I hear someone say those two words: *déjà vu*. That old French magic still gives me the shivers.

Can I Sit With You Too?

If I Had Grown Up Online: Reflections on Bullying

~~~~~~~~~~~~~~~~~~~~

Amy Looper

Elementary School

When I first heard about Ryan Halligan, a thirteen-year-old boy who committed suicide, I was sad to learn about yet another child taking their life because of bullying.

Then I watched the Frontline show Growing Up Online, and was completely horrified by new information Ryan's parents shared. They had contacted some of Ryan's friends, to get answers to their many unanswered questions, and learned that Ryan had visited a website that teaches kids the best way to commit suicide, based on a personality test.

I couldn't shake the profound sadness out of my head for days after watching the Frontline special. I had a rush of vivid and unexpected memories about a kid I knew in elementary school, back in the 1960s, who repeated first and third grade.

Everyone knew who she was and teased her relentlessly, calling her stupid, retard, dummy, the usual hurtful stuff some kids will say to those they see as different, or as lower on the proverbial playground food chain.

Some of the teachers chimed in on this ridicule, which was even more abusive and shocking. They called her out in the classroom with snide comments, and made her stand out in the hall. This kid couldn't catch a break.

She was out for a week one semester, because her father died. Kids and teachers were nice to her for a few days, but eventually the taunting picked back up.

Then one day during recess, one of the bully boys came over and took the girl's jump rope. He quickly fashioned a hangman's noose over a tree branch. Then he grabbed this picked-on girl by the arm, threw the noose around her neck, and gave a big tug with all of his weight. He was easily twice her size, and when he jerked her up, she was swinging in a matter of seconds. Hung by her neck from a tree right there in front of everyone. Not one kid moved to help. I think they were all stunned.

She grabbed her neck with her hands to stop choking, and struggled to get free. Then the bell rang, recess was over, and the bully boy let go of the rope. The girl fell to the ground. A teacher came toward the big tree, but when she saw the girl fall to the ground, the teacher turned around and left the girl to pick herself up. No one helped. They all just filed back to class like nothing had happened.

That little girl was me.

What Ryan Halligan's suicide made me realize was that, if the bullying I endured as a child had been complemented by the resources of a twenty-first century online world, I too could have easily checked out the suicide website and—even worse—acted on it.

The thought shook me to my core.

Even though I was very lucky to have loving parents who guided me through my trying times as a child and saw me into successful adulthood, they still had no idea of my many sad and lonely days, because I couldn't articulate the full extent of what was happening, much less understand what I needed from them.

This is why I've dedicate my life's work to supporting kids in their technology-based culture, leveraging technology in every way possible, and creating positive content options. I want to be a lifeline to life skills for all kids, so they can learn how to confidently navigate this fast-paced world, and the myriad negative influences they face daily.

If you're a parent, teacher, or anyone else who simply cares about youth, you should watch Frontline's Growing Up Online at: http://www.pbs.org/wgbh/pages/frontline/kidsonline/.

Though Growing Up Online neglected to mention the many positive online options currently offered to kids, it is still an important eye-opener for offline adults.

Dodging Bullet

~~~~~~~~~~~~~~~~~~~~~

Laura Eleanor Holloway

Between ages six and nine at the time

Everyone just called her Bullet.

Blonde hair cut like a boy's—rumor was she had no mother,
Which seemed to explain the fact that her favorite toy was a hammer.
And not some hollow yellow plastic PlaySkool job that squeaked as you
      hit plastic pegs. No,
Bullet's hammer was the real deal,
Straight from Heckinger's, "The world's most unusual lumberyard."

That day, the six swings were full of hostages:
Twelve legs brown with dirt and sun,
Twelve tender palms freckled with stinging rusty equal signs,
Twelve open-toed shoes dragging despondent trails in the soft dry dust
      as Bullet made the rounds:

"Do you like me?"
Her hammer poised menacingly above timid knees,
There was only one way to answer the question.

Occasionally, as she moved down the line,
Someone would make a break for it and
Bullet, hammer-wielding Thor-ling,
Would chase them back to the swing set
And ask again:

"Do you like me?"
"Yes, Bullet."

I had a lot of time to think
While the other five children were lying to Bullet.

Didn't her father see from the window what his daughter was doing?
Why didn't he stop her?
Take away that hammer?

"Do you like me?"
"Yes, Bullet."

As she got a few children away, I whispered to Kathy:
"The only way we're gonna get to leave is if someone tells her No."
Kathy's eyes grew wide in horror:
"But...she'll hit you!"
"I know. Shhh."

"Do you like me?"

The Weirdest Kid in the World

~~~~~~~~~~~~~~~~~~~~~~~

Mike Adamick

Third Grade

The crazy began in third grade. Mrs. Rudolph, my teacher, was circling the classroom with a new assignment, cackling about its difficulty like a grade-school Elmira Gulch. Only instead of riding a bicycle and threatening to put down Toto, she pointed out that she had spent all night conjuring up the most horrendous quiz we could imagine.

"Good luck," she sneered, leaning over my desk.

I was wondering why she singled me out specifically—did I need it? Jesus, was I the dumb one? What did she mean?—when I saw it. Her nose. Her nose started like a lump of fleshy pudding between her eyes and then suddenly sprouted forward as if someone had installed a tiny stick in the taste treat that was her main feature. The stick came to a sudden stop and seemed to split at the tip. The forked effect was frightening. Considering how big of a witch she was, it didn't necessarily surprise me that she had what amounted to two pointy noses, but it was still discomforting to behold them up close. I stared too long, a moment too much, and Mrs. Rudolph recoiled a bit, as if to say, "What?" So it didn't put me in her good graces when my hand instinctively reached for my own nose, to feel whether my proboscis split as well.

She put her hands on her hips and huffed, "And what exactly are you doing? That's not polite, you know."

But I couldn't help it. I was enthralled. My fingers felt around my nose, examining the tip points. Just like Mrs. Rudolph, I had two nose tips as well. Only mine were buried beneath a layer of flesh like a normal person.

It quickly became an uncontrollable habit. Whenever I saw Mrs. Rudolph, my hands jumped to my nose and felt for the two tips. At some point, as the year progressed, I began to feel sorry for the poor woman, as I hounded her with habitual nasal mimicry. She began to avoid looking in my direction, as I would spend hours staring at her nose while examining my own. Most children picked inside their nose. I felt mine up. But her nose had cast a spell on me, and it became something of a ritual to enter the classroom, glance at her face, and then put my hands to my own, assuring myself that my nose hadn't visibly split over night.

It was my first quirk, my first small, nascent bit of what would become a lifetime devotion to crazy.

A few months later, I entered the class to find Mrs. Rudolph with her back turned, engaged in a conversation with another broom-rider. I was devastated. Didn't she know so much depended on our new routine? If I couldn't see her nose right away, I couldn't feel my own and then I couldn't walk the exactly three steps to my desk, circle it once and sit down so that both of my butt cheeks touched plastic at the same time. Didn't she know that my quirks were reproducing like rabbits and that her oddly-shaped features were the cause of my burgeoning personal torment? I stopped in the doorway as other students pushed around me. But I couldn't move. I craned my neck, hoping to catch a glimpse of her nose.

"I know you're there, Michael," she said suddenly, her back turned. "Just take your seat."

My feet were glued to the floor.

"Go on," she insisted, "I'm not in the mood for your little antics."

My foot lifted off the ground and simply fell back in the same place. It tried again. And again. But I was motionless. I could see my desk. It was only three feet away. But I couldn't make it. I couldn't move.

It would become a familiar feeling throughout my life, this inability to function if my quirks and superstitions weren't first sated. Some people can't leave the house, for instance, without checking the coffee pot or making sure the lights are off. A lot of people can't go to bed without first checking to see whether the stove is turned off. But how many people have to touch each dial, ensuring they are all in the off position before crossing the room and flipping the light switch exactly twice? I've been playing in a Sunday softball beer league for seven years now, and I have yet to step on the third or first base line, and every time I jog into the outfield, I am forced to pick up a clump of grass and toss it into the air to test the wind—even on perfectly calm, windless evenings. Flying is of course a nightmare, as the entire flight hinders on whether I can utter an exact phrase exactly six times in the time between the first engine roar and take-off. That kind of responsibility is daunting.

But it gets really embarrassing when I have to knock on wood.

A lot of people subscribe to the superstition that if you don't knock on wood, whatever fate-tempting statement you just made may well come true, or not. A lot of people don't know, however, that you have to be precise in the administration of this superstition. What if, for instance, you accidentally knock on wood more than the usual two times?

In my view, if you accidentally knock three times, you have to knock one more time to make it an even four. But four, oddly enough, balances out two knocks because it is the polar opposite—it is double two knocks, in other words, and therefore carries more weight. So if you accidentally knock on wood three times instead of two times in the very beginning, you have to just go ahead and knock on wood six times to make the number round and to cancel out all the ill-effects of having an accidental knock in the first place.

But did you know that six is part of the devil's notorious numbers, 666?

You have to go higher than that—but you can't stop at seven because it's an odd number, and you can't stop at eight because it's double four and therefore evil. Ten seems too even for some reason, so why not just go up to twelve? But wait a minute—how many knocks have you done now?

Was it twelve or thirteen?

Friday the thirteenth?

You can't risk that.

Just keep going to fourteen, but wait—there's a four in it. Fifteen…no. Sixteen? Please, it's double of eight, which is double of four—you might as well just give up, go lay down somewhere and wait for the Fates to destroy you.

So there you are—approaching twenty knocks on wood because you said something a little too gloating, too wishful or boastful.

Once, I knocked on wood 522 times.

The worst part is when I'm around someone else who knocks on wood three times. It is apparently my lot in life to even things out for these imprecise imbeciles. At a work party a few years ago, a coworker knocked on wood three times. My boss was just a few feet away, and because I was relatively new to the job, I didn't want to appear as out and out loopy as I usually am, and so I didn't run to a nearby table or door frame in search of wood. Rather, I relied on the one allowable substitute for wood: my head. I stood there holding a drink with one hand and tapping my head with the other.

As I was approaching thirty knocks, my new boss nudged me on the shoulder, and asked, "Um…are you okay?"

"Whatever do you mean?" I replied, trying to play it off by using my finger instead of my knuckles. I lost count, however, and had to start over. At the time, I imagined I simply appeared thoughtful, tapping my reddening pate with a finger as if pondering something important. In retrospect, tapping yourself 58 times in the side of the head probably doesn't come off as intelligent. I remember thinking that if I didn't wind up fired or institutionalized the next day, my new coworker owed me his annual bonus.

Almost every time I knock on wood or check the stove or skip lightly over the third base line, I am taken back to standing in the classroom doorway in third grade, waiting for Mrs. Rudolph to turn around so I could see her nose. The bell rang and she still hadn't turned around, which meant I couldn't touch my own nose and then find my desk.

It was a pivotal standoff—we were nose to nose, so to speak. And to this day I wish I had backed down. I wish I had simply returned to my desk and forgotten all about this fledgling system of twitches and quirks. Sadly, Mrs. Rudolph turned first, pointing a finger in my direction.

"Don't you dare—do you hear me?"

And there it was—her nose. It was a two-pronged beacon, pulling me toward a lifetime of regret. I tried my best, I really did. But there was no stopping my hands. They jumped on their own accord to my face and felt the tip of my nose, as Mrs. Rudolph shook her head and sighed. She went to her desk and pulled a slip of paper out of a drawer.

"Try explaining this to the principal," she said, while I fondled my nose, hopped over the doorway, being sure to land on my left foot, and took a long, precise route to the school office.

Ski Bum

~~~~~~~~~~~~~~~~~~~~~

Jennifer Byde Myers

Age nine at the time

Lena was beautiful, which was no surprise to anyone who had ever met her family. Her mother was stunning, with glossy black hair, olive skin, and a hint of old world Catalan in her speech. Lena's father was handsome, tall and lean, and blond in a grown-up way. He only spoke German to Lena. It was nearly impossible for me to make eye contact with the piercing green eyes of Peter, her older brother; he was also tanned, and had thick hair that whispered across his forehead.

They were an athletic family, whereas mine was not, unless you counted the Sunday morning bike rides to the donut shop. Lena's family hiked and biked and surfed and climbed things. Lena's mom played tennis in her crisp white skirt and pale pink "real" Polo shirt. Her shoes were spotless, and the sweat that dripped down her forehead never seemed as nasty as the sweat the rest of us got from the Southern California sun.

I loved being friends with Lena because we were always moving when we played together. We roller-skated and skateboarded and ran to the beach and back. I was giddy when her family invited me to go skiing for the weekend.

I was pretty good at skiing. Not "I ski in Austria in the winter" good like Lena and her family, but I could hold my own, having been taught well by an uncle (thank God for extended family). I had the "right clothes" and there didn't seem to be any shame in renting skis. I packed my things into the smallest bag I could find so I wouldn't take up more than my share of space in the trunk of the car.

Lena's family picked me up on a Saturday morning while it was still dark. I wore a beautiful blue coat and had an angora headband to keep my ears warm. Black snow bibs were in fashion and as it turns out Lena and I had the same ones! (In fourth grade, there is nothing better than being twins.)

It was a beautiful day and we sailed down the easy and medium difficulty runs. The sun shone brightly and I could see my freckled self reflected in Lena's sunglasses. I had forgotten my sunglasses. Well, I hadn't really forgotten them. I just didn't own any sunglasses. I was the only person on the mountain without sunglasses.

We went into the shop so I could buy some. I had $15.00 in my pocket and there were so many pairs it was hard to choose. In fact, it became increasingly difficult to choose because every pair was at least $18.00. We waited at the bottom of the ski run for Lena's parents (who took the black diamond runs the entire way, of course). Lena's father handed me a five dollar bill and told me to keep the leftover change for a soda. I bought the cheapest pair and had less than one dollar in change.

We skied and skied until we met Lena's parents and brother for lunch. I sat next to Peter, sipping iced tea and crumbling saltines into my ski slope chili; I wanted to add salt to it, but was so self-conscious that I couldn't stand up to look for any. Peter looked right at me, touched my nose with his thin tan finger and said "Wow. You are totally going to get burned. Dude, you should put some more sunblock on."

Sunblock. *Crap!*

"Yeah. I should."

"You brought some right?"

"Uhm, yeah. I mean no. I put some on at home." This was technically not a lie, as I had, in the past, put on sunblock at home. I hadn't done it that day, of course, before skiing with the "I only look better with a tan" family who had probably never even purchased sunblock.

My mom was going to kill me. My dad, a skin cancer survivor, was going to be sooooooooo angry with me.

I would just go buy some. Oh, wait, no, I wouldn't, because I had spent all of my money on sunglasses.

Lena's mom and dad got up from the table. Her mom said, "Oh, good. You put sunblock on at home, so you will be fine." Then she and her shiny black hair and her unfreckled, golden face took off down the hill, followed by her Coppertone husband.

We skied until the lifts stopped running. I had been in the glorious springtime sun of the Southern California mountains from nine a.m. until five p.m. Eight hours without any sunblock on my pasty whitey-whiterson face.

For some reason, we didn't spend the night at their cabin. Lena's dad was a doctor; perhaps he was called home. So we went back down the mountain, and slept in the back seat of the car. It was dark when I arrived at my house, and, exhausted, I went straight to my room and to bed.

I woke up the next morning with second degree burns all over my face. My nose was one giant blister. My forehead sported a clear demarcation from the angora headband; everything below the band was covered with 7000 more freckles per square inch than the top half. I could barely open my mouth.

My mother gasped when she saw me. My father was thankfully already on his Sunday morning bike ride to the donut shop.

"What happened? Why didn't you put on your sunblock?" My mother wanted to call Lena's parents and berate them for allowing me to get this sunburned.

I was so embarrassed and ashamed. I had taken my sunblock out of my bag so I wouldn't seem like someone who needed a lot of things just to go overnight. I hadn't put on sunblock before we left because I didn't want to smell like sunblock in the car and have Lena's brother think I was weird for putting on sunblock while it was still dark. I didn't want to ask for more money to buy sunblock and make it seem like I was trying to get Lena's family to buy me things; and besides I had basically lied to Lena's parents. Why would they want to buy something for a liar?

My burns were so bad that I was out of school for two days, and spent more than a week, maybe two, peeling and bleeding and cracking.

Because I was vain and insecure that one day, for the rest of my life I will have small thin lines running down my chin, reminding me to put on my sunblock—and my confidence—before I leave the house.

Instruments

~~~~~~~~~~~~~~~~~~~~~~

Lisa Lucke

Age nine at the time

Mrs. Winton had barely finished forming the phrases "school assembly" and "music recital," and my nine-year-old heart was already pounding. I tracked her every move as she made it clear that, "Yes, families were invited." This meant that I would actually be up on the stage, violin nestled under my chin, my hand carefully sliding the thin bow over the taut strings, just the way Mrs. Winton had taught me to do.

I'd only been playing for a few months, like everyone else in the fourth grade with their newly-chosen instruments, but I was absolutely sure of my abilities. Every Wednesday afternoon, instead of going to last recess, I walked to the cafeteria for music. I was proud of myself, and most of all, I felt important.

At the sound of the three o'clock bell, I ran the two blocks to my house, where I found my father mowing the lawn. "Dad!" I shouted over the grinding noise of the push mower, "We're having a recital in two weeks and guess what?" My dad rotated the mower at the end of the long row and managed a breathy response.

"What?"

"Family gets to come and it's in front of the whole school and it's at night!"

"That's great, Lisa. Go call Mom and tell her the good news."

The days flew by, filled with extra practices after school, and rehearsals that filled in every detail, from where we would sit and whom we'd sit next to, to reminders about how to dress. One by one, Mrs. Winton fine-tuned our weaknesses with gentle admonishments, as if we ourselves were the instruments and she the player. Finally, at the end of two weeks, we were ready. I couldn't believe that this unlikely instrument, the third I'd tried in as many years, the one my mom said was my great-grandmother's passion, would be the one to propel me into the spotlight, and out of the ordinary.

I had thought the same thing about the accordion two years before, in second grade. Mr. Carlotti, a seemingly ancient man, found my two best friends first. They were sisters, and lived just a couple doors down from me. One Saturday morning, the seemingly ancient man trod door to door in our neighborhood, looking for prospective students. Chrissie and Debbie's mom said yes, and before he had even left their porch, the girls sprinted down the sidewalk, past the cranky neighbor's house that separated us, and flew up my porch steps. I opened the door to their frantic chattering that I must get my mom to say yes to accordion lessons, though just what an accordion was I didn't exactly know. When Mr. Carlotti reached my door, after old Mrs. Tadblink shooed him away, the polite gentleman in the dark brown suit got lucky again.

The three of us, Mr. Carlotti's only students, wedged into his tiny office in the basement of the public library each Saturday morning. We had exactly four lessons before what I now realize was Mr. Carlotti's likely overdue passing. I wasn't so much sad for poor old Mr. Carlotti as I was for me. I wanted to get good at something, and the accordion was different, so different than any other instrument most kids played. For me, different meant special, and special meant better.

I tried again the following year, during third grade. I took piano lessons from a spinster who lived across town in an aging Victorian. She had a slobbering monster of a dog who rested his mouth, complete with gloppy tennis ball, between my knees as I played. Miss Ricky hugged me the first time I entered her house, and every time after that. She hugged me goodbye, too. She may have even hugged me after each song—I just remember her thin, yet surprisingly strong arms squeezing my shoulders in a lovely vice-grip, and her nervous, happy voice prattling all the time.

Miss Ricky's corrections came in the same tone as praise: soft and encouraging. She ended each lesson by playing anything I wanted, and without exception, I chose one of Joplin's rags. I loved to watch Miss Ricky's bony shoulders and arms and fingers vibrate up and down and that silly look on her face that resembled a smile but may have just been the natural slope of her wrinkled, oval face. I also remember that when she played she seemed to be somewhere else—somewhere I wanted to be, without even knowing why.

For three months I played at Miss Ricky's house, which ended up being the problem. My parents decided that without a piano of our own at home to practice on, I was not making any real progress, and therefore, lessons were pointless. The decision took me totally by surprise, and of course, I disagreed. In my mind, and definitely in Miss

Ricky's, I was doing just fine. Besides that, I enjoyed the lessons, which were more like a trip to a carnival than work, and most of all, Miss Ricky *needed* me. Why else would she insist on showing off the endless upstairs rooms of her house each week after our lesson ended, and keep introducing me to the relatives who stared out at her antics from behind dusty glass? How could I make my parents understand that progress really wasn't important to me, but spending time with Miss Ricky was? I couldn't, so I quit the lessons and reluctantly said goodbye to Miss Ricky.

But now, just one year later—under the direction of Mrs. Winton—I would reveal my musical talents to the world, with the violin.

At promptly six o'clock on a Friday evening in late October, Mrs. Winton stood center stage in front of the heavy velvet stage drapes and welcomed the assembled parents, relatives, and teachers to the Fourth Grade Fall Music Recital. Behind the curtain, my classmates and I sat in our assigned seats—me near the end of the third row, between two other violin-playing fourth graders. I knew I'd be able to catch a glimpse of my parents between pieces, and I was already imagining how proud they'd look. I wiped my hands on my jumpsuit and tried to stay calm.

At 6:03 p.m., the curtains parted a crack, and Mrs. Winton slipped back through, looking us over for the last time. As she quickly made her way toward the wings, we made eye contact, and she stopped just long enough to whisper one, simple sentence in my ear that remains with me to this day, thirty-three years later:

"Lisa, I want you to pretend to be playing."

With that, the curtain rose.

School Nurse

~~~~~~~~~~~~~~~~~~~~

Ken Putnam

Fourth Grade

I went to grade four at Brentwood Park Elementary School in Burnaby, British Columbia, in 1959. I was not a bright student; far from it. One day, while I was doing my usual best to avoid a question from the teacher, the PA system came on. It was the school secretary, summoning me to the nurse's office. The school nurse was a nice lady, and since I did not feel sick and other kids got called to see the nurse all the time, I was not worried.

When I knocked on the nurse's door, a male voice said, "Come in." I went in, and was met by a really old man—probably around forty years old—who introduced himself as Doctor Someone. The good doctor wore a light scruffy beard, thick glasses with large black rims, a plaid sports jacket, and, of course, a tie. On the desk was a pipe, because this was back when adults smoked just about everywhere.

The doctor asked me some questions: "Ken, do you have brothers and sisters?" "Where do you live?" What's your favorite color?" "Do you have a pet?"

I answered all the questions to the best of my grade four ability and was feeling pretty good about the whole deal. At least here I was getting some answers right, unlike in my classroom.

Then he hit me with the big one: "Ken, I'm going to give you some colored pencils and I would like you to draw me a picture of a man." I began to panic. I froze with fear. I couldn't draw a straight line, let alone a picture of a man. He told me he was going to leave the room and come back in about ten minutes. He left.

I wanted to jump out the window. I had no idea why this guy wanted me to draw a picture of a man. What had I done? Why was this happening to me?

I did know one thing: the results of my artistic endeavors were going to be very important to my future. A pass or fail on my drawing would no doubt be the catalyst for something great or terrible. So I picked up the green pencil, then the red, followed by blue and yellow. My brush-cut head was wet with sweat, and my fingers sore from squeezing the pencil so hard. My little brain was roaring at one thousand miles per hour.

The door opened and the doctor came back in. "Well, how did we make out, Ken?"

"Okay, I guess," I said, and I handed him my picture. A slow smile came across his face and then a soft chuckle. He put down the picture, looked me in the eye and said, "You know, Ken, I don't think there is anything wrong with you at all, you're going to be just fine."

The doctor was right. I'm fifty-eight years old now. In 2005 I retired after thirty-four years with the Royal Canadian Mounted Police, and now work for the Yukon Department of Justice.

And the picture? Well, I drew the doctor: complete with his pipe, plaid jacket, glasses, and beard.

All God's Children

~~~~~~~~~~~~~~~~~~~~

Victoria Laraneta

Fourth Grade

I grew up in a small Midwestern town. We were, I suppose, middle class folks; we lived on the "right side of the tracks" by several blocks. It never seemed to matter that much, but I was aware that there were kids who lived up the hill in houses that were bigger and newer, and that other kids lived across the tracks in smaller houses that didn't have big yards. Though our homes were different, at school we seemed to be much the same, and we were all pretty good kids.

I have always had friends from both sides of the tracks. My grandmother taught me to love everyone because we are all God's children.

Even so, I remember that I still seemed to feel sorry for the kids on the "wrong side of the tracks." One girl in particular, Sophie, was in fourth grade with me. She always looked like she needed to shampoo her hair, and her clothes were not so pretty. And, unfortunately, her last name sounded like "bottom," so you can imagine all the teasing she received.

I always left school with Sophie, walking together part of the way home. Then she would turn right and walk her six blocks over the railroad tracks, and I would walk straight home another four blocks. We walked to and from school every day, even in the winter when the snow was piled up as high as a tall giraffe's butt.

One warm rainy spring afternoon, we left school together as usual. We had only gone three blocks, just before Sophie should have made her turn, when we were accosted by some sixth grade boys on bicycles. They said mean, horrible things about Sophie, and then they teased me, asking me why I would want her for a friend.

Sophie looked at me and her eyes filled up with tears. She looked so sad and scared, and well, I just couldn't take it anymore. I folded my umbrella and took a swing at the biggest boy, and got him right on his fanny. I told him to get away or I would bonk him on his head and then run back to school to get the principal. He grabbed me, but I broke free and swung at him again with my umbrella. I missed him that time, but he decided I might hit him again so they just called us more names and then rode off.

We were very scared and crying by this time, so we ran through the rain all the way to my house, until I was pounding on the side door. My grandmother let us in, and as she toweled us dry with big fluffy towels, I told her the story. She said, "Good. I hope you smacked him a good one. Sometimes God's children are hard to love."

Sophie was supposed to go right home after school since both of her parents worked and she had siblings who would be waiting for her. But Grandma called her mother at work, and asked if Sophie could stay for a while, if we would give her a ride home in the car after dinner.

Grandma gave us a piece of her homemade bread with grape jam and a glass of milk, and talked to us for a while. When we had calmed down and had bellies full of Grandma's snack, Sophie looked at me, smiled, and said, "Thank you."

I said, "That's all right. You're my friend."

Face to Face With the Banality of Evil

~~~~~~~~~~~~~~~~~~~~~

Anna Dalprato

Age nine at the time

Translated by Lea Cuniberti-Duran

Winter 1941: So many years have passed, but the moment in which I realized I was "different" is still vivid and alive in me. And even though that discovery was traumatic at the time, today, it is the source of my true wealth.

My elementary school was in a small rural village in the north of Italy. One afternoon on the threshold of winter, I sat in a classroom under the supervision of volunteers, making socks for soldiers who were fighting in Russia because Mussolini had dragged Italy into the Russian war. Four little girls and four sets of knitting needles worked the thin and rough woolen thread.

We felt particularly committed to supporting our troops, those young men who were so far away, fighting in a frozen and inhospitable land. I worked very hard with my small and unskilled hands, filled with pride, and carried by a feeling of love for my country.

But that day, Elvira, a girl who used to play with me on the playground and who knew my family well because my father was her family doctor, stood up in front of the others and said, "Anna cannot work among us! She is the daughter of the enemy, therefore she is an enemy of our soldiers."

Murmurs swept among the girls, followed by surprise and dismay. Elvira went on to explain, to erase any doubt that remained: my mother was not just Russian but also Jewish.

Night seemed to enter the room and I ran away in tears, screaming, "I AM ITALIAN!" I ran all the way home, but I didn't speak with my parents then or ever about what happened, because I knew what Elvira said was true.

My babushka, Sophia Szulkis, who lived with us until the beginning of World War II, was a Russian Jew who left her country with her four children after her husband died. They arrived in Palestine in 1916.

My mother, Ester Fira, got a scholarship to a school in Berlin, Germany, when she was fourteen years old, and stayed on in Europe. She completed her studies at the University of Bologna, Italy, where she met my father. They married in 1931.

At the time Elvira denounced me, my mother had been an Italian citizen for years, and was culturally and emotionally connected to her new country. She was a respected member of her community, and was the pharmacist in the rural village where I grew up—although she was forced to leave her job in 1938 when Mussolini issued the first anti-Semitic laws. As far as I know, she never experienced hatred in our village; I remember her being very loved and esteemed.

So why did this little girl harbor such horrible feelings? I knew that they were not shared by most of the people we knew; perhaps it was something talked about in her family? I don't really know what moved this girl to speak up: was it anti-Semitic sentiment, or my mother's roots in Russia, an enemy country where our soldiers were dying?

As I picked up the pieces of my life, I didn't feel different, only sad and lonely, like other children who get excluded and marginalized by their peers. I started to live in the world of my imagination and of books, and fell in love with the righteous world of the ancient Greeks. But I still felt lonely, and even a bit guilty, because I never returned to those afternoon meetings to knit socks.

A few questions have stayed with me, and now, years later, I can ask: Why didn't the adults in the classroom intervene? All decent people! All quiet! The war and subsequent social upheaval were overwhelming, but a single word could have explained to the other girls that it was not shameful to be different because of race, religion, nationality, or lifestyle. Sadly, people rarely stand and speak up. Most would rather stay quiet, and follow the flow.

I truly believe that it is through these silences and omissions, through negligence that it is possible to marginalize, condemn, and even persecute.

Hanna Arendt wrote about the Shoa (Hitler's campaign to exterminate the Jewish people) as the "banality of evil," in which evil's casual servants are our neighbors, and the people with whom you stand in line at the grocery store. These everyday people are closed in their silence, in their own need not to rock the boat, so they comply with the status quo. This attitude closes people inside their own made-up world of "normal." It makes them reject diversity.

Diversity should be considered a wealth, a source of comfort, and an opportunity for growth for the individual as well as the community as a whole. This is my hope, and with that hope I am making peace with these old memories, which today I can finally share.

Mobil Oil Cans

~~~~~~~~~~~~~~~~~~~~~~~~

SK Knight

Fourth Grade

Fourth grade girls,
squashed Mobil Oil cans
scrunched on the soles of their feet,
had the power to stomp in tight angry circles,
stand two inches taller and feel connected,
not fall off the face of the earth,
dragged off the earth by fear.

"I know all about your father!"
said the snot-nosed crew-cut kid.
"I know because my father is a cop!"

Mobil Oil cans on both my feet
gave me the idea for one quick second
that I'd like to smash his face straight
and hard into the ground,

and then I'd fly off the earth, free.

But, afraid of his father, of him,
of the thing he knew about me,
I scrunched down on Mobil Oil
and walked away, making damn sure
they didn't fall off my feet.

A Special Education

~~~~~~~~~~~~~~~~~~~~~~~~

Gwendomama

Age nine at the time

I had a horrible sore throat. But I knew that if I called my mom, I had better be really sick. I waited until each swallow caused more agony; the razor blades of saliva being forced down. I finally went to the office, where the nurse called my mom. It may have been my tears, or it may have been the obviously sick look of hot red cheeks and swelling eyelids. Whatever it was, I was taken right to the family doctor.

Four days, two blood tests, and countless baby aspirin later, we found out that I had "mono," i.e., infectious mononucleosis.

I had never heard of mono, but I was sick, and not in an enjoyable, "hang out in my parents' room watching TV and being served tea and toast and pudding" sort of way—more in a "feverish, lump-swallowing, headachy and swollen" way.

I was miserable with mono for one week. Then I became miserable with boredom.

I was still too sick to go to school, but no longer sick enough to be content with the confines of bed rest. My mother tried to help: She brought me find-a-word puzzles, complicated origami projects, new books—and pudding. I was suddenly allowed unrestricted access to the television, but found daytime TV before the advent of cable booooooring.

I was desperate to go back to school after two weeks, but the doctor said that my spleen was still freakishly enlarged, and it was too risky for me to go back to school. When I complained, I was told that if I was knocked down, pushed, or worst of all, punched, I could bleed to death. I wondered why, if my spleen was that much of a problem, the doctor didn't just remove it. But as I didn't relish the idea of being cut open, I kept that thought to myself. I did laugh out loud about the "being punched" comment, though, and assured the doctor that I had never gotten into fisticuffs with anyone, ever.

He condemned me to two more weeks of staying home and "taking it easy" (running laps up and down the stairs and jumping on the bed when my mom went to the store and would not notice the chandelier shaking under my room). During this time, my brother, who went to the same school, would bring me my homework and notable nuggets of school gossip or scandal. One day he came home and told me that everyone was talking about how I had the Kissing Disease, and how everyone knew I had kissed someone to get it.

Huh?

Most certainly not.

Brian McCann had pinned me against the climbing structure and planted one on me, but that was in second grade, two whole years ago!

My mom confirmed that mono was called the Kissing Disease, because it was most prevalent and contagious among college kids, and they kissed a lot. I was satisfied with her answer.

Later that week, my best friend Kirsty was visiting and told me that most of the kids were saying that I had to have French kissed someone to get mono, and suspects' names were circulating. Brian McCann would have been the prime suspect, but since he was also the one who delivered the Divine Truth about mono germs being passed through French kissing, he was out. Brian suggested that I had kissed either Herbie, the kid who always wore flood pants and who never smelled quite right, or Mister K, the janitor.

All of this information was delivered to me in snippets via Kirsty the week before I was to return to school. But I didn't worry too much; Brian McCann was no rocket scientist, and his accusations were ridiculous. I didn't even feel the need to find out what a French kiss was, to deduce if I actually had, accidentally, French-kissed someone.

I was allowed back to school with explicit instructions from the doctor: I was not allowed to walk the four blocks to school, or attend PE classes for the remainder of the school year. My doctor was still concerned that I would take a dodge ball to the spleen. Or fall on the way home. Or get punched.

My three best friends surrounded me on that first day back, giggling and welcoming me excitedly.

My teacher Miss Spranger smiled at me and said, "So, our little Gwendolyn is back from having the Kissing Disease!"

The class erupted into laughter. I was mortified, but somehow remained smiling. My beloved teacher had betrayed me, but surely I could take a small joke?

Before we were excused for PE, she asked if I wanted to stay in the classroom or come watch my classmates participate in PE. The idea of being benched in front of all those kids was horrible, so I chose to stay in the classroom alone while the teacher went to the lounge for a smoke break.

After a week of this, I got bored and started wandering the halls looking for something more interesting.

At one end of the building was a door with a lot of noise coming from behind it. I stood on my tippytoes, looked in the window, and saw the most interesting pieces of wooden equipment and toys I had ever seen. And the room was full of children—little tiny ones—who were all different in some way from the children I'd seen at other preschools. I scanned the room, intrigued, when suddenly the door opened and I almost fell into the room.

"Can I help you?" asked the pretty young teacher who had opened the door.

"Umm, well, uhh—could I come in and meet the little kids?"

"SURE!" she practically shouted. She walked me around the room, introducing me to each child as if they were—normal.

"This is Jenna. She really hates her new stander and she is feeling mad about that today. This is Vincent. He just learned how to roll himself over! This is Alison. She really wants to say hi to you!"

I looked down. Alison was grinning wildly up at me, her chin glistening with fresh drool.

I checked her hand for drool and then grasped it as I had been taught, years ago. I shook her hand while she grinned even more wildly and made some dog-like squeals of delight. For some reason, this was okay.

"Uhh, nice to meet you, Alison, uhh—should I—can I—read you a book?"

After that, Miss Avery asked my teacher if I could spend my PE periods in her classroom, "helping." I was thrilled to be invited on a regular basis—being able to help made me feel important, and there was something about that room, and those children, that made me want to be there. I felt grown up. I felt pride. I wasn't sick and I hadn't French kissed the janitor. I was a junior teacher!!

Every Tuesday and Thursday I got to spend nearly an hour helping the lone teacher and her eight awkward students. Together, we celebrated such victories as audible utterances, rolling over, self-feeding, and hauling one's prone body up a soft foam ramp.

One day, not too long after I started my new gig, I came back to the classroom one day to find Brian McCann already back from PE, sweaty, energetic, and wild-eyed.

"Soooooo, Little Miss Priss, where were *you* during gym class today?"

"You know I can't do PE anymore," I hissed back.

"So where were you? I saw you hanging out with the retards."

I was ashamed. I was caught. I wasn't sure what my offense had been. I just knew I had been caught doing something terrible.

"RETARD! RETARD! Gwen is a RETARD!"

Since the teacher was not yet back from her smoke break, he had the momentum of anarchy behind him.

"RETARD, RETARD!" Half the class joined in, just arriving and not even knowing why they were chanting along.

I felt so much shame. I was embarrassed. I had broken some sort of social code; one that I had not even realized existed until then. Then again, I had been in remedial math since my month out of school. Maybe I was retarded.

I went to the nurse and asked her to call my mom. I told her that my spleen was hurting and I needed to go home.

She gave me a strange look but made the call.

The next day, I stayed home. When I returned, things were worse. Snickers and covert taunts of "retard, stupid retard, retard head" were the fun of the schoolyard. My brother wasn't there. Kirsty was nowhere to be seen. Almost everyone got in on the action. A foot shot out—someone tried to trip me as I ran away. Suddenly, the silly idea that anyone would ever want to punch me became frighteningly not silly.

Then in the afternoon, came PE. I had to make a choice. I didn't want to let Miss Avery down, but I didn't want to be teased anymore.

Then again, I didn't want to lose the sense of superiority I had over these mere children in my class. While they were off playing kick-ball, I was a teacher's aide!

I had another full month of skipping PE to go. I had to decide.

I helped Miss Avery for the rest of the year.
I wasn't able to continue helping after that.
The following year I asked to switch schools.

Can I Sit With You Too?

Love Note

~~~~~~~~~~~~~~~~~~~~

Wookie

Age ten at the time

I'm a loner and have been since nursery school. Even the idea of having a friend is completely foreign to me. My class is an amalgamation of the "smart" kids of the entire school district and we are all attending a full-time daily "enrichment" program. It is ninety minutes away by bus, meaning I leave home at 7:05 a.m., well before sunrise, for much of the school year.

I am two years younger than all of my classmates. My entire wardrobe consists of jewel-toned jogging suits and I am crowned with a bright red afro (thanks to an unfortunate haircut). I listen to the other kids obsessively but when I try to be social with them, even they can tell I'm mimicking. They think I'm a freak. In a classroom full of kids that were supposed to be like me—I'm still a freak.

When we start taking wood shop, I discover that I really enjoy working with my hands. I've begged to be allowed to take weekly wood shop class with the boys, because my other choices are home economics and art, and I already know how to bake and use a sewing machine, and I have no artistic skill whatsoever. Reluctantly, the wood shop teacher grants me permission to join his class when my homeroom teacher intervenes on my behalf. I am delighted.

Wood shop is apparently a proving ground for the budding adolescent male, a place where jocks are suddenly on equal academic footing with nerds. The teacher belongs to the jock group. I can tell this by the way he stands and which students he jokes with, but beyond that the social nuances of the setting are lost on me. For once I'm so different that I'm left completely alone. A girl isn't worth the time of the jocks or the nerds.

We do different projects to learn to use the different tools, moving from hand tools to power tools and then onto the machines, giant sanders, saws, lathes. My success is mediocre, but I don't care! It's new and I love the smells and sounds and solitude of the projects. After a few weeks, the teacher tells us to prepare on graph paper a design to cut out on the jigsaw. Something with some curves and some straight edges, and he'll approve the designs before we're allowed to copy it onto a piece of wood. I spend the next week tracing and retracing the same design: a musical eighth note, with the note itself in a heart shape. I plan to carefully sand it and color several different samples of the design for myself, trying to decide on what color will look nicest hanging on my bedroom wall. I painstakingly draw more than a dozen of them, trying to get the perfect balance of heart-to-stem, the heart shape proportional and not too fat, not too thin, the stem not so thick as to throw off the balance of the picture, the tail on the eighth note gracefully curved and angled.

Finally, the morning of the class arrives and I eagerly wait my turn, wait to have my design approved so I can pick out a piece of pine from the scrap bin and start working. I watch while the teacher nods and smiles at the jocks' designs, and sighs but approves the nerds' designs. I present my own colored master plan, on graph paper as specified, and wait.

The teacher frowns. His eyes narrow. I don't know how to read his reaction. Angrily, he gestures towards the drawing, "What is this supposed to be?"

"A love note!" I say proudly. I feel it is both clever and cute, and I am eager to learn how to use the jigsaw.

His jaw clenches. Then he crumples my design up, tosses it in the waste-paper basket, and tells me to sit at my desk. I'm too confused to cry while he steps into the next room—the art room—and briefly speaks to the teacher. I am shortly steered by the shoulder into art class, where I spend the remaining six weeks of the semester making a coil pot out of clay, my cheeks burning with shame because I still don't know what I've done wrong.

The incident was never mentioned again.

Can I Sit With You Too?

Schooltime Story

~~~~~~~~~~~~~~~~~~~~~

Mariann Vlacilek

Fifth Grade

I went to grade school in Huntington Beach, California, in the 1940s. I felt so out of place, plain and unnoticed. I was very thin, with an olive complexion, and long, straight, dark hair. I felt like I was all arms and legs. I was born in Panama and my mother was Castilian and French, ergo the complexion that is now called "Mediterranean." I grew to envy all the girls at school with light skin and blue or green eyes. One girl in particular had red hair and green eyes, and I though she was the most beautiful thing I had ever seen.

Sometimes, I was called racial slurs. At one point, this actually led to an altercation in the nurse's office. I am a very laid-back person but enough was enough! This was so very hurtful and damaging to me that I became even more self-conscious, and suffered a great loss of self-confidence.

It was a custom at my school for members of the graduating class to compile a list of underclass students' traits that they admired and would like to have, and publish the list in the yearbook. Imagine my utter amazement and disbelief when my name appeared on their list not once, but twice—it had been unanimously voted that I had the most beautiful eyes, and hands! Me, the fifth-grader with the long, dark hair, and olive skin. Me!

This was somewhat of a turning point for me. It made me realize that I wasn't an unnoticed nobody, and that there were things about me that were admirable. I should have learned from this, but the previous hurts were so deeply embedded that I bottled them up for years.

I didn't fully realize the lesson of being listed in the yearbook at the time. It didn't hit me until some thirty years later, when I looked in the mirror one day, and that little girl seemed to reflect back at me. At that moment I learned from her that, although thought of as pretty, I was also someone of value. That changed my life.

Every so often, I think back and am once again thankful and amazed that those older girls actually wanted something of mine that they didn't and couldn't have!

Years Before I Was Allowed to See R-Rated Movies

~~~~~~~~~~~~~~~~~~~~~

Shannon Des Roches Rosa

Age ten at the time

I spent fifth grade in a segregated geek/G.A.T.E. class on a regular elementary school campus. We were quite sheltered compared to our "regular" campus peers, which meant that our complete obsession with anything naughty had limited information feed lines. My friends Mike, Miho, and I had to bounce everything off of each other.

Like everyone else in our class of delineated dorks, we were given lots of self-directed free time with which to develop our supposedly impressive intellects. This means we were forever fooling around, telling proto-L33T Dolly Parton jokes that ended with the victim spelling "55378008" on their calculator, making naughty cartoons and comic strips, and modifying the lyrics of every song we learned in class, to see who could come up with the filthiest result. I will not reproduce our efforts here, but please know that there is a reason I smirk every time I hear the lovely Quaker ditty Simple Gifts.

One song had, however, been pre-altered for us. Somehow, we came into possession of the following lyrics for that classic dance hall tune, Ta-ra-ra Boom-de-ay:

Ta-ra-ra Boom-de-ay
I met a boy one day

He gave me fifty cents
To go behind the fence

He pulled my panties down
Then pushed me to the ground

He counted 1-2-3
Then stuck it into me

My mother was surprised
To see my belly rise

My father jumped for joy
It was a baby boy

Every ten-year-old we knew, and even those we only knew of, could sing this lovely tune celebrating rape and teen pregnancy. It quickly became one of our standards.

Mike, Miho, and I decided that, given our considerable free time, we should give the song a comic strip counterpart. We named the protagonist Selena, made her a teenage prostitute, and set about illustrating her adventures. She was insatiable, our Selena. Mostly she would meet a man and then discreetly walk out of a frame, but there were times when her hunger demanded something more substantial, such as the planet Saturn. I can only imagine what my parents would have thought had they had seen these still very childish drawings, which contained no penises (eww!) or indeed anything more graphic than a long shot of Saturn going up Selena's skirt between two verrrrry widely spread legs.

This may sound horrifying, but I don't really think it was. We were not actually interested in the sexual aspects of our songs or cartoons, only in the thrill of dabbling in absolutely forbidden themes. (And cursing a *lot*. That was also a thrill.)

I myself was so completely clueless about sexuality and sex—I knew that a man could put his penis in a woman's vagina, but not one jot else—that I didn't realize the reason I liked climbing the two-story firefighter-style pole on the jungle gym was because every time I did it, I had an orgasm. (Who had ever heard of orgasms?)

I even tried to talk to Miho about it: "When I climb that pole, my butt itches. Does that ever happen to you?" Miho said no, as she preferred to stay on the ground and play soccer, but she did ask her mother, who said that she sometimes got an itchy butt at high altitudes. Since her mother spoke only Japanese, I am guessing something got lost in translation, both coming and going. I couldn't get up the nerve to query my own mother, because we were Catholics, and if something pleasurable came out of wrapping—not even rubbing—my legs around that pole and climbing, then it had to be bad.

My friends and I were more naive than perverted. And we were still quite innocent: we spent recess playing games like Statue Maker and trading stickers. I was fond of using my transparent red visor cap to catch the bees that gathered pollen from our playground's clover. The three of us liked to suck nectar from the honeysuckle blossoms that grew on the playground fence. We were neither warped nor damaged, nor were we exposed to "bad influences." We were simply curious fifth grade children with both too much and too little information.

No-Win Scenario

~~~~~~~~~~~~~~~~~~~~

A. A. Matin

Age ten at the time

Gym class. Most people's memories seem to revolve around dodgeball. While I have been hit with, and in turn, pelted many a classmate with those red rubber balls, my most vivid memory is of another game: Capture the Flag.

There were about fifty of us in the fifth grade. The gym teacher set the game up on a huge soccer field. In order to compensate for the size of the field, each team had three flags. Early in the game, my friend Pasquale and I decided to run across the field together, capture one flag, and throw it back and forth to each other as we ran back to our side.

We made a break for it. I snagged a flag and turned around. I looked over to Pasquale who was running with me. Then I looked ahead and saw a straight shot back to our side. I didn't even think about tossing it to Pasquale; I just ran as fast as I could, and we made it back. I apologized to Pasquale for not throwing it to him, but he didn't care because we got the flag and were not tagged.

Later on someone got the idea for a bunch of people to run over at once and ambush the other side, in the hope that one person could break through. I didn't think it was a good plan—but went with it. The other team was prepared, and set up a wall of defense that captured us all.

Our "holding pen" was a pole on the edge of the playing field. We were allowed to string ourselves together by holding hands to form a chain. So many of us were caught that we extended nearly all the way onto our half of the field. If one of our teammates could tag the person at the end of the chain he would free us all. Some guys took their shirts off so that they and the next person in line could hold it between them, to make the chain longer.

I refused to take my shirt off. I was very skinny and extremely self-conscious about my body. I did not feel comfortable, plus I knew I would be picked on and ridiculed.

But it did not matter. My entire team turned against me for refusing to take off my shirt. Everyone was upset, saying that I was not a team player and was refusing to help. The fact that I had captured a flag was inconsequential.

I didn't want to get insulted for being skinny. Instead I got insulted for not being a team player. Most would call that a "no-win" scenario. But that was not the case. No one else captured any flags. We won the game. And it was all because of me. That may have been lost on my classmates—but I still remember it, twenty-five years later.

The Absolute Clear-Headedness of Mrs. Rutland

~~~~~~~~~~~~~~~~~~~~~~~

Louis E. Bourgeois

Fifth Grade

You pass hall after hall on the red tiled floor until you pass the trophy case and enter the math class. You place, very consciously, an extremely yellow pencil in the pencil holder on your desk. As you wait for instructions as to what you are to do, the awareness that everyone in the class is essentially your enemy takes hold, and you wish a hurricane would come through and wipe away the fear. This is life in the fifth grade in a public elementary school, and this experience in the fifth grade in a public elementary school is no different from any other person's experience in your position. It has always been the fifth grade for the sake of being the fifth grade. It's timeless, and there's nothing you can do about it.

The yellow pencil reflects the gleaming rays of light coming down from the ceiling. Mrs. Rutland tells you to pick the pencil up off the floor. You look down at the floor but there is no pencil and you say to Mrs. Rutland that you didn't drop a pencil on the floor, forgetting that you should have taken the pencil on your desk in the pencil holder and put it on the floor yourself. But your paltry logic is, of course, what does you in, and will continually do you in.

The logic stands firm for a moment, but Mrs. Rutland simply tells you that you better pick the pencil up and show it to her. This is a second warning and somehow you just don't get it. For some reason you just can't bend down and simply do what she is asking. You are a rebel, and so a second time you tell Mrs. Rutland that there is no pencil on the floor. You claim to yourself that you are undergoing a serious injustice. You know you're in the right, you feel you'll be rewarded, and you start to feel all warm inside, honey warm. You know the Principal will be a logical man as you walk down the hall with Mrs. Rutland's hand on your shoulder.

She announces what you did in a few straight lines. Mrs. Rutland has no need to seal your fate; she knows you'll do it for her. She knows and this is why she asked you to pick up the pencil. Somehow she knew you were the one less deserving than the rest. Call it the mark of Cain if you will. But in your case the question of what you did is not in any respect relevant to anything.

The Principal has you in his domain. You know the Principal; you've seen him around before and never had much of a problem with him. He surely looks friendly enough, though you haven't actually talked to him. But now he seems different. You notice the Principal's pock-marked face, you notice how much he seems to like Mrs. Rutland, you notice how sharply his tie is tied, and you notice the neck of a whiskey bottle sticking out of the desk drawer. The paddle hanging on the wall, with several holes drilled into it, actually fills you with hope and relief. At least Mother might not find out.

You have to sit in a large old cushioned chair, and are told not to leave the room while the Principal goes outside. After he shuts the door you begin to make little whimpering noises, and you absolutely think you will go out of your mind. In your few moments alone, you consider your possible choices, and, of course, the only real thing that matters is that you make a deal without Mother knowing. This is about all the bargaining power you have, and you weep, and you smile, and you weep, and you smile, and you weep, and you smile.

But you keep condemning yourself; you're a revolutionary, an individual, and so forth. You keep defining yourself and making it worse with every remark you say to the now-returned Principal. You will not accept the fact that the pencil was lying on the floor. You will not agree to that, even though that's all the Principal wants. You even go so far as to talk about "kid's rights," and bring in witnesses from the class. Your inflammatory speeches nearly have the Principal rolling on the floor hysterically. He asks, what the hell is wrong with you? Do you think you're a superstar? Do you think you're Alexander the Great? Do you think you're a god?

You've been with the Principal for half an hour and the bargaining is about over. He feels the need to tell you how important it is to listen to your teachers. He tells you how much about life you don't know. He tells you how important it is not to disappoint your parents. And every time you think you're off the hook, he says he ought to call Mother, and you sink back into your unimaginable gloom. You've never felt this way before, and you've been around, you're in the fifth grade.

Can I Sit With You Too?

You make the deal and perhaps it has something to do with a call from his wife while you sit in the chair with all of your misfortunes running over. After the phone call his face is severe, and you start slipping, slipping, and slipping. Thinking of the injustice no longer helps; in fact, you think maybe the injustice was all in your head. The Principal knows what you are thinking, and he knows he has you because you want it too bad. So it's ten licks with the paddle and five days of recess detention, and an apology to Mrs. Rutland, and you count your lucky stars because Mother will not find out—and you hardly feel the air-swishing licks across your butt.

Can I Sit With You Too?

Treading Lightly Back to Middle School

~~~~~~~~~~~~~~~~~~~~

Alison Chino

Age eleven at the time

In general I have not been the mom who couldn't stand it when her kids moved to another stage in life. (Not that there is anything wrong with that mom.)

At times I have thought that there must be something wrong with me because I am able to walk away from milestones such as the first day of kindergarten, without crying. But honestly, I have tried to simply celebrate whatever stage my children are in. I loved my babies as babies, but I don't wish they were still babies. I embraced having three toddlers under five at home, napping on the couch, and never showering. I appreciated that we didn't have to be anywhere at a certain time, and that I basically had complete control over my children's choice of friends—and their choices about everything else.

Then my oldest child started kindergarten. I was excited that we were done with being home and had entered a new era: elementary school. It seemed as though every year after that, I had another child starting kindergarten. And even though my youngest is only two, I feel as though he will start kindergarten any minute now.

But this year there has been a little kink in my plan to always embrace the next stage of my children's lives, because one of them finally reached a stage that I just wasn't excited about. My oldest son, Cole, has started middle school. Every day, he walks into the same building that I walked into during my first year of junior high. He's playing the trumpet. I played the trumpet. It's his first year to have a locker. I still cry when I think about trying to remember my locker combination.

We took Cole to and from school for the first few days of middle school, but now he's riding the bus. Which is better, because I don't have to break out in hives when I drive to the school and remember my middle school days.

Last spring we went to the school for orientation. I was walking the halls with Cole and I said, "Yep, Cole, right there. There's the spot where Mama had her very first nervous breakdown. That's right. That desk right there in what used to be Mrs. Moore's class."

Cole looked at me with an expression that clearly did not mean, "I feel you mom. I'm just so sorry."

Like Mrs. Moore, he did not understand the plight of an eleven-year-old girl who was being made fun of daily by the boy who sat right across from her, because if Mrs. Moore had understood, she would have used her almighty powers to move that boy to the other side of the room.

When I say I was being made fun of, I do not mean the kind where people say to you, "Oh he is just flirting with you." I know about the kind of teasing that is really just flirting. That's what this boy did to other girls. But me, I was mocked, made the butt of all jokes and made to look like the complete idiot that of course I already believed I was because I could not ever ever get my locker open on the first try. Or manage to get to class with everything I needed. Or come up with a science project that would please the likes of Mrs. Moore.

Usually I managed to get all the way inside my house before I would cry. I would take deep breaths as I slowly walked the road from the bus stop to my house, and up the stairs to my blessed bed with the Holly Hobbie bedspread. "You can make it," I would tell myself.

But one day, I couldn't make it. I didn't even make it out of third period. I cried so hard that I actually hyperventilated. Which finally made people notice that I was being hounded by a mean boy for the entirety of every science class. And here's the thing about middle school. You don't ever want anyone to take notice. Your parents, yes, and your close friends, maybe, if you have any. But not the rest of the world. To them, I was just trying to be invisible. So, yes, the mean boy got in trouble. It was a long time ago, so he even got spanked. Which I *never lived down*. Mrs. Moore finally moved him, disdainfully. And I spent the rest of the year trying harder and harder to disappear into the nonexistent spaces between the lockers.

When Cole and I got home from his orientation, he told his dad that I was completely crazy and could his dad please take him to all of the rest of his middle school events instead of Mom? When we filled my husband in as to why, he said with complete nonchalance, "That's funny. When I was in seventh grade, I got spanked for making fun of a girl until she cried." I lost just a little bit of respect for him right then and there. Respect he will not regain until he finds that poor girl and apologizes.

Can I Sit With You Too?

Which he cannot do, because he doesn't remember her name. They never do.

The good news is that I don't think that Cole is going to repeat my middle school experience. And I know this not just because he is a boy. I know it because on the first day of school I picked him up and when he got in the car he was chewing on something. So I said, "Hey, what's in your mouth?" To which he replied, "My locker combination."

And because he is the kind of boy who would actually *eat* the only piece of paper he has with that sacred information on it, I had to give him a lecture right then and there about *never* making fun of girls.

Pick Your Battles

~~~~~~~~~~~~~~~~~~~~~

Madeline McEwen-Asker

Age eleven at the time

I spent my formative school years at a Roman Catholic Convent. As a direct result of that experience, I have a vast knowledge of bullying behavior. Unlike my own children's enlightened school, my school had no anti-bullying policy.

Bullying, like any other unpleasantness, had to be endured, was a cross to bear for the greater good of our immortal souls. I was an ideal victim: a head shorter than my peers, round, and freckle-faced. My immortal soul shriveled during target practice.

I made regular visits to the confessional each Saturday morning to cleanse that immortal soul prior to Mass the following day. I would detail my laundry list of offenses before the priest. At the end, he would often ask if there was anything else I wanted to ask. I took this as an invitation to moan about my poor benighted lot in life. I gathered that the priest had little experience of childhood, or maybe it was just too long ago, as his advice was to tell my persecutors that I would pray for them. It sounded like sage advice to me and I took the first available opportunity to put it into practice.

I didn't have to wait very long.

Sadly, the priest's advice did not bring about relief. As I dusted myself off from the latest pulping, I decided that an alternative plan was required. I had tested my mother's advice, "ignore them," but that had proved fruitless. I had followed my sister's advice, "walk away," but ended up running at warp speed on short little fat legs.

I finally ended up with a mentally satisfying option: whatever they said, I would agree with them, whole-heartedly, good-naturedly, and enthusiastically, followed by a jolly good simper. The balm of sarcasm would maintain my sanity.

"Hey McEwen, come over here so I can join the dots on your face!"

"Oooo please do, that would be delightful. Do you have a pen? Here you can borrow mine. I wish I was as talented an artist as you are."

It didn't work at first, but I kept trying.

The leader of the pack was one wizen and twisted Geraldine, the bane of my life. She was a cross between Dick Dastardly and Cruella de Vil. I instinctively knew that if I could just get her to crack a smile, I would bend her to my will, or, failing that, slip under her radar. Her torments were regular and unfailing. Apple pie beds, stealing tuck boxes, hiding mail, public humiliation of every kind that could be devised by the truly unloved.

It wasn't the pain of being tripped up in line and sprawling on the floor that bothered me, it was the following punishment from the staff for this misdemeanor offense: "McEwen! Get up this minute and cover your embarrassment! This kind of wanton spectacle will not be tolerated. Go to the chapel, say twelve Hail Marys, and pray for humility, modesty, and chastity."

The days passed slowly and became weeks. One term followed another but I still bobbed above the Plimsoll line. Then, during a holiday period, I happened to break one of my arms, again.

"But I can't go back to school! I can't write!"

"You can still learn. You can learn to write with your left hand."

So I returned to school, with a cast. I was miserable to learn that there was no escape from school, so miserable that I hadn't the will power to submit to Geraldine any longer. I kept a very low profile, lizard-like, but she still sought me out.

Triumphs when they come, are often small, not a fireworks display, merely an ever so slightly damp squib.

"So there you are, McEwen. Licking your wounds no doubt."

"Hardly, I don't like the taste of plaster of Paris."

"You look…grumpy."

"That's right. I am grumpy. Very grumpy. Very grumpy indeed."

"Good, I can give you something to be really grumpy about, then."

I saw her take something out of her skirt pocket. My brother's old catapult, purloined from my room!

"Want it back?" she weaseled, dangling it before my eyes.

Lizards can sometimes move very quickly. I snatched the catapult back and shoved the single end down my cast to scratch the itchy bits, saying, "Ah that's much better, how thoughtful of you." Then I whipped it out with a cloud of old dried skin cells.

"Here, you can borrow it for a bit if you like?"

Geraldine didn't sneeze but her nose wrinkled.

I should like to say that she stopped bothering me after that incident, that I won, but I think it was more that she lost interest, or perhaps found a new and more interesting interest.

Now that I am a grown-up person, I suspect that ghastly Geraldine was also homesick. For all her bravado, she had no friends, only cohorts. Perhaps our powerlessness in an adult world provoked her to try to gain control, and revenge. I often think that resilience and persistence are the flip sides of the same coin.

Maybe she did, too.

Will You Go Out With Me?

~~~~~~~~~~~~~~~~~~~~~

Sarah Dopp

Age eleven at the time

His name was Stephen Lawful, and he was the only boy in the fifth grade taller than me. His best friend was Joey Marcus—the shortest kid in the class.

Stephen looked like a teacher. He had perfect hair, parted on the left side and swept over his forehead with gel so that it never moved. He wore a long, tan trench coat and carried one of those big black umbrellas that you only see at golf courses. He talked with a lisp, used big words that I'd never heard before, and always said "please" and "thank you," even to the janitors. When he and Joey walked next to each other—like they did every recess—the other kids laughed behind their backs about how silly they looked with their two-foot height difference. But they were best friends anyway.

Stephen, Joey, and I were Smart Kids, and in our school, that wasn't really a good thing. They put us in small classes, always with the same other Smart Kids, and they kept us away from the rest of the fifth grade. They called us the "best and the brightest," and were proud of us. Unfortunately, all that meant to us was that two hundred other fifth graders wanted to beat us all up.

The Smart Kids always sat together at lunch, even though it was embarrassing, what with Stephen being six feet tall, Joey being four feet tall, and me being lanky and gawky with big glasses and clothes my mother picked out for me. We all just kind of looked like a circus. The rest of the Smart Kids were weird, too. To pass the time, we picked on each other. We were good at making each other feel worse.

But Stephen was always nice to me, and he made me feel like a real person. I started to think about him a lot—as in, more than I thought about my other friends. I thought about him on the bus, and in class, and during dinner, and before I went to sleep. He was so tall. So nice. So sweet. So cute.

And I wondered if maybe he thought about me a lot, too.

I didn't tell anyone about how much I liked him. I knew they'd laugh at me. Everyone thought Stephen was way too weird, and I wanted them to think I was cool.

A few weeks went by, though, and I realized I couldn't stop thinking about him. It made me nervous. I felt like I needed him. I was writing his name on my notebooks and staring at him whenever I saw him and—omigod I had such a massive crush on Stephen that it was starting to eat up my insides and turn my brain to mush.

Finally, I confessed the crush to a few of my friends, during a sleepover. They giggled and teased me a little, but they saw that I was serious and they agreed that Stephen was nice. We all decided that I needed to ask him out.

So I ripped out a piece of notebook paper and wrote him a letter in my neatest, prettiest handwriting, with a pink pen:

Dear Stephen,

Will you go out with me?

Love,
Sarah

I was so nervous when I wrote the word "love" that I almost spelled it wrong.

I folded the letter up into a square and wrote, "To: Stephen, From: Sarah" on the front.

I gave it to him on Monday morning, when we were all outside before the bell rang. My hands were shaking and my friends were staring at me and all I could manage to say to Stephen was, "Here."

I didn't pay attention to any of my morning classes. All I could do was stare at the clock.

At lunchtime, a bunch of people sat between Stephen and me. Everyone knew about the letter, and that he still hadn't answered me. Both our faces were bright red.

I poked Jen, who was sitting next to me, and asked her to ask Derek to ask Joey to ask Stephen if he read the note. Five minutes and lots of whispering and giggling later, Jen turned to me and said, "Yeah, he read it."

I sat there for another five minutes, not really sure what to do. Finally, I poked Jen again and asked her to ask Derek to ask Joey to ask Stephen if he had an answer. There was a lot more shuffling, whispering,

Can I Sit With You Too?

giggling, and talking. Ten minutes passed and no one was talking loud enough for me to understand. My chest was tight, my knee was bouncing uncontrollably, and I couldn't eat my spaghetti.

Finally, after forever, Jen turned to me and said, "He says he doesn't think of you that way. He says he thinks of you as a sister."

I was quiet for a minute. "So, um, is that a no?" I asked.

Jen turned around and whispered some more. It took another five minutes. Lunch was almost over and people were starting to dump out their trays. My heart was aching and I was trying not to cry.

"Yeah," she finally said. "That's a no."

It took me a month of avoidance and frustration and fantasies and anger and crying before I could hang out with Stephen again. All through middle school, and even all through the beginning of high school, I still liked him. I still wished we could be boyfriend and girlfriend. He was still the nicest guy I knew. But he never opened up to the idea. Eventually, I moved to another town and didn't have to look at him anymore.

When I was twenty-one, exactly ten years after I wrote him that letter, I had lunch with Derek from middle school. We were talking about our lives and the people we knew, and I asked what everyone was up to. He started listing people off, "Jen's a marine biologist in Florida. Joey went to Harvard for Engineering and he's working on his Master's now."

"What about Stephen?" I asked.

"Oh, he ran off to LA with his boyfriend and no one's heard from him for a while."

"His boyfriend?" I asked incredulously.

"Yeah," he said. "He's gay. Wait. You didn't know that?"

Can I Sit With You Too?

Cheater, Cheater, Pumpkin-Eater

~~~~~~~~~~~~~~~~~~~~~~

Sabina Sood

Age eleven at the time

"I dare you to cheat on your math test." The gentle breeze blows her words away before they reach my ears.

"What?" If my words aren't enough to portray my puzzlement, my scrunched nose, half-opened mouth, and furrowed eyebrows are. Did she say, "cheat"? How will cheating on my math test make me worthy enough to be accepted into her circle of friends?

"I double dog dare you to write down all the test problems and give them to me," she taunts. Who does Kristina think she is, besides the leader of the most popular group in fifth grade? As my flame of hope to join her group is snuffed, I turn around to leave.

"I *triple* dog dare you. You can't turn that down!"

My shoes squeak on the dewdrop grass as I pivot to face her. A smile tiptoes across her face as the other girls in her clique laugh.

She knows I know about the unwritten rules that bind every elementary school kid to the social ladder. Every kid keeps this rulebook tucked away in a corner of her mind until the day she outgrows it and passes it on to someone else. One of my friends passed this knowledge on to me when she graduated from elementary school, and during times like these, I wish she hadn't. This rulebook is the Bible of elementary school and not abiding by it makes ruining one's social life inevitable.

As I ponder her statement, I flip through the pages of the rulebook in my head. Here it is. Page 37, Rule #182: "If a kid is dared to perform a task, she has the choice to accept or refuse it. If a kid is triple-dog-dared to do something, she must complete the dare, or risk public humiliation."

If I refuse the dare, then word of my sin will spread like wildfire throughout the school, and no one will ever speak to me again. If I accept the dare and cheat on my math test, I will jeopardize my elementary school career. But that will only happen if I'm caught.

The next day, I enter my math classroom, my heart pounding and my mind searching—searching for the courage and reassurance that escapes with every breath. I accepted the dare and there is no turning back. My face tingles as shivers dart up and down my spine. Sweat trickles down my arm as I focus on one sustaining thought: I accepted the dare and there is no turning back.

Mr. Walshe reads the directions of the math test. Time creeps by. Tick, tock, tick, tock. After what seems like an hour, he finishes his speech with, "You have forty minutes to complete the test. You may begin."

We turn the page. One student taps his pencil on the desk in a rhythmic pattern. Another accompanies him as she hits the desk frantically with her shoe. Tap, tap, bang, tap, bang. As the other students scribble on their scratch paper and fill in the bubbles on their answer sheets, I grab my pen, turn my left hand over, and jot down the first problem on my palm. "If 3x+5=…" The sweat from my hand smears the ink. "If 3x+5=…" My hand quivers, causing even the prettiest handwriting to be illegible.

I cross out my mistake and find a clean part of my palm to begin again. "If 3x+5=20, solve for x." I glance up to see if anyone notices. Mr. Walshe types on his computer. The other students rustle their test papers and answer sheets. I look at the next problem, but I hear something as I bring the pen to my hand.

"Sabina, what are you doing?" Although he whispers, Mr. Walshe's deep voice penetrates the classroom. His tone drowns the paper rustling, and derails the pencil-tapping and shoe-banging harmony. As he stands by my desk, his shadow devours me. My heart sprints to catch up with my embarrassment. The blood from the pit of my stomach rushes to my head as my face boils. He grabs my test and tears it in half. My classmates murmur. I can't swallow and can barely inhale enough oxygen to stay conscious.

"Let's go talk in the hallway," he says. I can't move. My feet are glued to the ground. Guilt desiccates every drop of saliva in my mouth. It chains me to my desk. I struggle and finally break free from the shackles. The water that disappeared from my mouth now crowds my eyes and streams down my face. As Mr. Walshe crosses the classroom, I try to run, but my feet are anchors, they are maliciously enjoying every student's stare that pierces my ego and follows me out of the classroom.

As soon as the door closes, I ramble, trying to say anything that will save me from punishment:

"ThereisKristinaandtherulebookandshetripledogdaredmeIcouldntsayno."

I hate him. How can he embarrass me like that? It isn't my fault that I cheated on the math test. It's Kristina's fault for daring me. It's the rulebook inventor's fault for writing Rule #182. It's God's fault for giving me dreadful cheating skills. Why should Mr. Walshe punish me?

"This is your first and final warning, Sabina. I'll give you a second chance to take the test, but I will have to call your parents," Mr. Walshe explains. He returns to the classroom, leaving me alone in the hallway to think about what I have done.

The following day, I walk onto the playground and sit on the tanbark. Kristina and her group spot me near the swings.

"I heard Mr. Walshe caught you cheating," one of her friends snickers.

"How embarrassing," says another.

"Even though you failed miserably, having the guts to cheat makes you worthy enough to join my group. You can sit with us during lunch tomorrow," Kristina scoffs.

I turn around and walk away as her offer hovers in the air, waiting for the wind to blow it away.

Shoes Can Buy Me Love

~~~~~~~~~~~~~~~~~~~~~~~~

Brian Greene

Age twelve at the time

My family moved to Virginia Beach, Virginia when I was twelve years old and in the sixth grade. My father was in the Navy, and had just been transferred from Charleston, South Carolina, where we had lived for the previous three years.

We lived on the naval base in South Carolina, but in Virginia Beach we lived in town, among civilians. I was to find that life for a pre-adolescent was very different at a regular neighborhood public school compared to how it was on the base, at the Navy school.

On the base in South Carolina, there really weren't any established cliques amongst the kids who lived and went to school there. Of course you made friends with certain other kids and hung out with them more than others, but there were no exclusive groups to be part of or refused admittance to. Maybe this was because the society around a military base is so transitory and diverse; with the sailors getting transfers so often, families came and went on a daily basis, from all over the country, and sometimes from different parts of the world. We were all too transient, and too different from one another, for there to be much of a social pecking order.

It was very different in Virginia Beach. Upon joining the new school, I learned very quickly that my class was split into two distinct groups. There was a pack of about ten kids, half boys and half girls, who were clearly the elite. They made the best grades, the boys were the most athletic, and the girls were the prettiest. They sat by themselves in the cafeteria, and if you weren't invited to sit at their part of the table, you wouldn't dare go over there. All the rest of us kids were "the others," the commoners who took up space and were looked down upon by the elite crowd.

I had no great desire to get in with the popular kids, but what did bother me was that, even within the group of "average" boys and girls, I didn't seem to be making any friends—even after I'd been in the town, and at the school, for a few months. The other nondescript kids were generally friendly with one another, and many of them seemed nice enough. How come none of them were trying to befriend me, when I was one of them?

Finally, I decided to try to find out why none of them were friends with me. I asked a boy named Mark, who had done more than any of my other classmates to be nice to me. We were outside on the playground at recess, and Mark and I were standing off by ourselves.

I said, "Do you know why Marvin or Stacy or none of the other kids ever talk to me? I saw Stacy at the park near my house the other day, and when I went up to say hi to her, she walked away. People are always doing that to me. I'm not talking about Greg and Melissa and those kind of kids, I mean the regular ones, like us."

Mark looked like he was carefully considering how to answer my question. Then he came to a decision in his mind and he said to me, "I'll tell you the truth. It's your shoes."

"My shoes?"

"Yeah, they're Weos."

"Weos?"

"Yeah. You know how at the A&P grocery store they have some things that are like a sale brand? They call those things Weos. So to us anything that's cheap like that, we call it a Weo. You should get your parents to get you some Nikes or Pumas, or at least Converse."

"And that's really why kids won't talk to me?"

"Yep. A lot of them think you're a nice kid. They say if he would just get rid of those Weos, we would play with him."

It seemed that even among the "regular" kids, there were certain status symbols. I felt both confused and ashamed to learn that they were shunning me because I wore cheap, non-name-brand tennis shoes.

That night, before I went to bed, I told my mother about my conversation with Mark. I asked her if she could buy me some Converse, if we couldn't afford Nikes or Pumas. I made a deal with my mom, that if I mowed some lawns and put together a little bit of cash, she would pay for half of a new pair of Converse, and I could cover the other half.

I remember having a kind of creepy feeling when I bought the shoes and wore them to school for the first time. It was like I was buying the chance to make friends. In South Carolina, you made friends with certain kids just because you liked them and they liked you. Here, I had to wear a certain kind of shoe before any of my peers would consider befriending me. It didn't feel right.

Can I Sit With You Too?

But I forgot about all of that when, at recess the first day I wore my new shoes, Stacy—the same girl who had snubbed me at the park in our neighborhood—came up and talked to me. I'd had a crush on her since the first day I was at that school, and now she was flirting with me. I asker her to "go" with me about three days after that, and she said "yes." After we started going together she got her parents to buy her a pair of Converse that were the same color as mine.

Imagine This
(A Narrative on Bullying)

~~~~~~~~~~~~~~~~~~~~~~

lastcrazyhorn

Age twelve at the time

Let me set up a scenario for you:

Imagine first that you're a kid, maybe eleven or twelve, possibly thirteen. You have Asperger's syndrome, which means that your social skills are impaired already; plus you're a preteen/young teen, which means that the rules for your social world are constantly in flux. But, as of yet, you're not diagnosed; no one in your life ever heard the term "Asperger's," or understands what it means. As if that weren't bad enough, you're a girl who is more of a tomboy, who doesn't see the point in following the social rules or norms, either because they seem like a waste of time, or because you're mostly oblivious to their existence in the first place.

Most kids don't like you very much. You don't know why. Vaguely, you understand that there is something about your being that offends or bothers these kids. You don't know exactly what it is. You think that if you smile at them, if you laugh at their jokes (their very unfunny jokes), if you make a point to be really nice to them, then they'll see your effort and be friends with you. You think that if you can find a topic that you both can talk about, that you both like, then maybe you can have something in common and that'll help the situation.

They laugh at you a lot, these other kids. Sometimes you know why; sometimes you don't. They seem to be speaking a language different from the one you know. They use slang that's unfamiliar to you, because no one in your world speaks it. Your world consists of what you've learned from books (specifically fantasy and fiction and children's literature), games, adults, and perhaps a few highly specialized interests that you think are really cool, which no one else ever seems to "get" quite as well as you do. You start thinking that maybe you shouldn't mention

99

these interests, since they aren't very well received. But sometimes you just can't help it. It's something that's important to you; after all, other kids talk about what's important to them all the time, so why can't you?

Other kids bump into you in the hall. You try to be more careful so as not to bump into them, thinking it was your fault to begin with. You slowly start to realize that they are purposefully trying to hit you. Maybe it's a new kind of joke. Maybe not. Just to be safe, you always try to smile at them and say, "excuse me." They laugh, like you've said a joke, even though you're pretty sure that you haven't.

Sometimes they trip you and you fall. When they laugh, you think maybe you had a stupid expression on your face as you fell, or maybe someone said something funny that you missed. Sometimes you laugh with them, because after all, someone falling flat on their face is kinda funny, right?

Sometimes when you fall, you bruise your knee or cut your lip on someone's foot that got in the way of your fall. You try to smile, even though it really hurts, because maybe they can still be your friend if you show that it doesn't really hurt. Maybe you can show that you're one of them, because you're laughing and having fun, even though you are bleeding on the floor of the hallway.

Eventually, you might figure out that they are doing these things to you because they like seeing you get hurt. Somewhere between them putting a bee down the front of your shirt, setting fire to your backpack, stealing your backpack, flushing your inhaler in the middle of your asthma attack, pushing or throwing you down the stairs, spitting on or at you, giving you rope burns, drawing on your shirt in permanent ink, giving you the silent treatment at lunchtime (or just getting up en masse whenever you sit down), grading your homework wrong, and threatening your life by showing you a knife that they brought from home just to cut your throat with, you start to realize that maybe they really might not like you.

Slowly, you start to realize that those bullying and bullies videos your class watched a few months ago were demonstrating things that could really happen in your life. Who would have thunk it? So, you think to yourself, like anyone would after having seen those videos, that maybe you should tell someone about it. Either that, or the thought just never occurs to you as a viable option.

Say you try to talk to the principal about it. You ride a bus to school filled with these kids that don't like you. In fact, as you think about it, you've started getting diarrhea every morning before you get on the bus, just from worrying about what might happen that day. Most of the time your bus gets to school late, and your bus driver tells you to go straight on to class as fast as you can. So, you can't talk to your principal then, because the bus driver told you get to class as soon as possible.

All of the breaks in the day, when the kids push you and hit you going through the hall, are only about five minutes long. The halls are crowded enough without kids purposely trying to run into you; it should take two minutes to get down the hall but now takes four minutes. Plus, you have to go the bathroom on your breaks, because as it is slowly revealed to you, none of your teachers like you either, and they rarely allow you to take bathroom breaks. Apparently you are considered a difficult student, because you consistently have to ask a lot of questions just to know what's going on during class. Your teacher gives you instructions, but you aren't sure who they pertain to. Is she talking to all of the students in the class or just the ones who think that particular way? You don't know, so you ask.

You can't talk to the principal on any of your breaks. So you think, well, maybe I can talk to the principal at lunchtime. At lunchtime, after the food fight that seems to be only directed at you, you go over to your teacher, who is far off at her table, and try to ask her to let you go to the principal. The teacher, thinking that you're onto some new ploy to be allowed to go to the bathroom, or because just she doesn't feel like it at the time, says no, and tells you to go back to your seat and quit bothering her. When you leave her table, you hear them all start laughing and wonder to yourself who told the joke and what it was to make everyone laugh so hard? Boy, if you told that joke, people would fall down at your feet to be your friend.

You ride the bus home at the end of the day. You have to get to a seat fast, because otherwise, you'll end up standing or sitting in the aisle for the rest of the bus ride since no one thinks you really deserve to sit down. Plus, you have to carry on a French horn, and even though you might be a little slow socially, you can tell for sure that no one likes trying to accommodate that thing in their seat. You have no time to talk to the principal because if you miss your bus, you're stuck at the school even longer, and school isn't really that great, so why be stuck there longer?

Eventually, either you realize that if you go to the principal, the other kids will see and really will follow through on that threat to come to your house at night and hang you from your front tree; or else you do manage to see the principal and he either:

1. Doesn't do anything.
2. Doesn't believe you.
3. Calls you overly sensitive, or
4. Does something, but tells everyone who got them in trouble to begin with, resulting in your getting beat up by an entire crowd of kids, instead of just one or two.
5. Or some combination of the above.

Now, the kids who aren't actively trying to hurt you or embarrass you don't do anything to you, but sometimes they sit back and laugh while some other kid fills up an entire wall with spitballs while you crouch on the floor during the lesson.

There isn't anyone you can talk to, because either they're like the principal and don't believe you, or they call you overly sensitive and compare your situation to their days of woe, explaining that what you're really doing is building character, because, you see, you really don't know how it feels to be bullied and they do.

Every time you walk down the hall, either someone trips you, laughs at you, hits you, or whispers behind your back about how shitty a human being you are. In fact, sometimes everyone whispers and laughs at you as you walk down the hall. They say things like, "Hey what is *that?* Is that an *It?* Naw, it's a *Shit.* Hey *Shit!* Wanna blow me?"

"No," another one answers, "you wouldn't want *that* to blow you; think about what kind of diseases you'd get if *that* touched you. Bleah."

In the meantime, you start writing essays that are centered on themes portraying your violent death, which your teacher awards with A's, saying things like, "Wow, creative, but make sure you work on your handwriting next time."

One day, you decide that someone has just pushed too far; that, throwing your inhaler in the toilet was bad enough, but throwing it in a toilet full of poop was just a little too much; so you hit someone back after they've inflicted months of suffering on you. Instantly, the principal is called or the teacher sees it, and you find yourself on lunch detention for a week—or better yet, you're suspended and have to see the school counselor for a month, in order to work out your more violent feelings and the ways in which it might be better to handle yourself, should a situation ever arise again.

Or, say you try to hit someone and you don't get caught, but everyone laughs it off and starts calling you a freak, or rather, a nervous and crazy freak—and hey, you remember that one time when the nervous freak tried to hit me? Yeah, that was a laugh riot, wasn't it?

Can I Sit With You Too?

Imagine that everyone you try to tell laughs you off, or gets you in deeper trouble when they try to do something about it. Imagine that you have teachers who give you bad grades on purpose so that they can call you up in front of the class and show the class how "stupid" you really are. These same teachers also find great pleasure in not letting you go to the bathroom, even when you're really sick, because it's obvious to them that you just need a little toughening up.

Imagine that during PE, when you're not losing the game and people aren't throwing basketballs directly at your head just for the heck of it, you're instead sitting on the floor drawing your name in your arm with a sharpened pencil. Imagine that no one sees—or if they do, they don't say anything.

Imagine that this goes on, day after day after day. Imagine that once every twenty to thirty minutes someone either hits you, kicks you, calls you "Shit," laughs at you—or does all four. Imagine that you still think that agreeing with them will make them suddenly like you. Imagine that these are good Christian kids who go to church with you and either stand back and let all this happen, or are the ones doing the worst things to you.

Imagine that every time you try to fight back, someone either overpowers you, or you get caught and are in trouble. Imagine that every time you tell someone about it, they just tell you to grow up and get over it. Imagine that you tell the cop at your school and he tells you to quit bugging him and get out of his hair. Imagine that when you're at home, you start cutting or burning your arms just for the sake of feeling something, since it seems that unless people can see physical evidence, then it didn't really happen. Imagine that you ask trusted people for help and they ignore you and laugh.

Imagine that you start sleeping in a box on top of your bed for, say, six weeks, because it's the only time you really feel safe. And your mother thinks it's a just phase. Imagine that you start sucking your thumb again, as well as coming down with pneumonia. Imagine that you start pulling out your eyelashes and eyebrows, and all your parents do is get mad at you for making yourself look bad. Imagine that you suddenly realize that all there is to life is to hear the laughter of other kids while you hurt and no one helps you, no matter how much you smile or laugh with them.

Imagine that you have sleepovers with your teddy bears because no one would want to come to your house anyway. Imagine that for an exercise in your computer class, you have to make a spreadsheet with the names and ages of your ten best friends, and you have to use the names of your cousins from both sides of your family just to make up the difference.

Imagine that it's like this every single day. Imagine that you start dreaming of ways to commit suicide. Imagine that this goes on for more than a year; more than two; more than three. Imagine that every day of your teenage life is like this.

What do you do?

Ella, Enchanted

~~~~~~~~~~~~~~~~~~~~

Suzanne LaFetra

Age twelve at the time

Jorge strummed his blonde wood guitar on the hotel patio. He swaggered right up to the table where I sat, crunching a *taquito de pollo* drizzled with cream, flanked by my parents. I leaned toward him, his tight silver-spangled pants and mustard-colored mariachi suit bright in the Mexican sun. He looked me straight in the eye, and launched into a song that seemed to be breaking his heart. *Yo soy un hombre sincero...*

I was twelve, and enchanted. It was Holy Week in Puerto Vallarta. California was still groggy with winter, but Mexico was wide awake, fragrant, and rioting in color. Scarlet and magenta bougainvillea commingled, dripping over gleaming black balconies of twisted iron. Thick white-washed walls hid interior courtyards, filled with cooing birds and cooling palms.

I watched bright parachutes soar over the Pacific. I ate clams for the first time and crunchy curls of fried cheese dipped in smoky salsa. I devoured Gone With The Wind, perched poolside in a black bikini, legs slick with baby oil.

Back home, the foxiest boy in the sixth grade was Tim Morelli. I had thought that if I did the right thing, acted the right way, maybe he would invite me to his fort, clasp his St. Christopher medal around my throat, ask me to go steady. But a couple of weeks before my trip, Tim had invited me to meet him after school at the bluffs, in a hideout under the eucalyptus trees. I pushed my bike up the craggy, crusty hill and waited in the shade under tangy leaves, my heart thumping.

When he arrived, Tim jammed his grimy hand into my underpants and wormed it around. I squeezed my eyes shut, lips pressed together. The going steady would come next. A ring, maybe. I waited. Footsteps crunched through the leaves and he pulled out his hand. His two friends, Wally and Dave, elbowed each other, and Tim grinned.

I pedaled my lime-green Schwinn home as fast as I could, thighs on fire, tears streaming into my ears. No medal, no gentle kiss. After that,

Wally and Dave regularly ambushed me in the janitor's closet. They wrestled me to the ground, then groped and grabbed at me. "Gusto," they shrieked, mimicking a popular beer ad, and twisted the tender tips of my breasts. "Go for the gusto!" Each time, my nipples were purple for days.

But in Mexico, there were wide grins, low bows, a door swept open. And what does the *señorita* desire this evening? While Jorge strummed, I sipped my virgin strawberry daiquiri and imagined his mouth clamped over mine, what it might feel like to have that black mustache prickle my lips.

I was safe, high on my vacationer pedestal, with a moat of chlorinated water, Hawaiian Tropic Cocoa Butter, and my mother's watchful eye keeping me from harm.

At home, though, the boundary between child and woman was unsecured. On weekends at my dad's house, my older step-brother regularly terrorized me in the middle of the night, fondling my breasts with his dry hands, masturbating in the dark while I scrunched into a ball. Another guy started out as a babysitter, and we jumped Parcheesi pieces around a board; but after dark, the game changed; a slobbery kiss, a teenage hand cold on my belly, reaching, pushing.

"Don't tell," they all said, and I was ashamed, so I kept quiet. I figured I deserved it; that's what happens to girls with breasts already as big as their mother's, who dream of kissing mustached mouths, who are desperate to wear Tim Morelli's cheap ring.

The lip-glossy clear-eyed girls in magazines, the Susan Deys and Marsha Bradys, swung their hair and grinned. They didn't look scared. They wore gleaming white swim suits, slim bodies just right; no scraggly wiry hairs sprouting, no purple stretch marks, no Oxy 10 in their medicine cabinets, no worn copies of Are You There God? It's Me, Margaret under their pillows. They were cool, possessed, sure, un-slouching, un-needing. Unlike me.

A couple of months before our trip to Mexico, I discovered a saddle-colored stain in my underwear. I was the first girl in the class to get my period, but I had seen the film strips, I knew that it was just men-stroo-ay-shun. I snuck into my mom's bathroom and pushed in a tampon. It felt foreign inside me, uncomfortable; I didn't feel like horseback riding or swimming, like smiling Kathy Rigby had promised in the TV ads.

That afternoon, I hid in my room, record player blaring, furious at my body's betrayal. I knew what was lurking across the border; more bruised nipples and slimy tongues, more grabbing and jerking.

Can I Sit With You Too?

My mom came in, asked how my day was, and the tears dripped off my jaw line.

"Oh, honey, whatever it is, we can fix it," she kept saying, stroking my hair.

"You can't," I cried, hanging my head. "Nobody can."

After a few minutes, she spied my balled-up underpants in the corner and understood. She straightened me up, looked into my face, gently. "You're becoming a woman."

On our last day in Mexico, Jorge again came to our table. He sang a lovely lilting song, closing his eyes, chin tilted skyward during the best parts. "In your mouth, you will carry the flavor of me..." Then he took off his hat, and asked my parents' permission to leave a small gift. "So that you have warm memories of my country," he said in perfect English. It was a cheap, too-big necklace, a slab of marbled stone hanging from a cord. I was awed. It was the same mustard color of his mariachi uniform.

A tiny ballerina danced every time I cracked my jewelry box open to look at Jorge's gift. I fingered the cool stone cradled in red velvet. But I never wore the necklace, didn't want to feel the weight of it around my neck, the press of stone between my breasts. I just liked knowing it was there, waiting for me.

The Cure of Nowhere

~~~~~~~~~~~~~~~~~~~~

Amanda Jones

Age twelve at the time

When I was twelve years old, the father of a girl in my class committed suicide in deplorably bad taste. On a fine Sunday afternoon, he suggested the family go to the movies. Excited, all four children and their mother drove downtown with him. There, outside the parking building, the father told the family to get out of the car, leaning over and kissing each of them as they did so. Not being a demonstrative man by nature, the family thought this act mildly unusual, but no one commented. They stood on the sidewalk and waited for him to park and join then on the street.

Instead, he took the car to the sixth-floor rooftop, got out, locked the door, and jumped off, landing in full view of his family.

The man was clearly disturbed, but the malevolence of his act stunned the community. In the full bloom of pre-adolescent ego-centricity, none of us knew what to say to Lucy Q, whose father had introduced domestic horror into our lives for the very first time. She was an odd girl to begin with, bony and skittish. She didn't perform well in class and she played no sports. I can't remember if she had any real friends, and though I had known her since kindergarten, she was not one of mine.

Naturally there was a tide of morbid pity that swept through the school, but in reality that pity translated into most of us avoiding Lucy Q, as she came to be known, mainly to distinguish her as, oh, that Lucy.

In truth, I was haunted by the suicide. My mind kept attempting to recreate the scene. What were Lucy Q's thoughts as her father hurtled towards her? Possibly, I postulated, she didn't see him until he landed, with that sickening thump, in front of her. What happens to a body that falls six floors? Was there an obscene amount of blood? Was the family spattered? But the question that none of us could answer was why anyone would do something so infinitely terrible.

I never spoke to Lucy Q about the "episode," as my parents referred to it. I could not bring myself to mention it in her presence, and when she talked about her father, she referred to him as "dad," and spoke of him as if he were still alive.

I never knew what possessed my mother to invite her on our vacation, mere months after the suicide. Of course it was something as basic as kindness, but surely, as I said at the time, she could have dropped off a smoked fish pie or offered to take Lucy Q to the pictures. But to invite her to share my grass hut for ten days on a tropical island without consulting me, well, it was ludicrous.

I had the impression Lucy Q was as appalled as I was, but her mother came to school to take her off for a passport photo, giving me a grateful smile as she left the room. I had no choice in the matter, and settled into ill-mannered acceptance.

The first few days of the trip were consumed with travel and adjusting to being in the tropics. My mother fussed over Lucy Q, giving me fraught looks when I failed to live up to her ideal of a hostess. Lucy Q and I did not talk very much. She kept occupied by reading Enid Blyton's The Famous Five series and watching the geckos that moved industriously over the woven sides of our hut. I wrote moodily in my diary and walked the island, which was a tiny South Pacific dot, a place of no consequence on the global map.

It was my first time in a developing country. There was poverty on the island, but a moderate, subsistence kind of poverty that seemed not to make the locals miserable. They were hefty and tattooed and their teeth were dazzlingly white. They dressed in cloth bound around their torsos, even the men. I remember this fact surprising me, that they could work their crops wearing a skirt. They smiled unreservedly and beckoned to me if I walked past their fields, handing me stalks of sugar cane that they had deftly peeled with their machetes.

There was a constant low current of excitement for me on that trip. It was years before I put a name to that feeling, but I believe it was the exhilaration of discovery.

Some days later one of the staff at the hotel asked if Lucy Q and I wanted to take a boat ride to an outer island to go snorkeling. Neither of us had snorkeled before, but we both agreed to go.

Although I was a strong swimmer, I was anxious about snorkeling, never having been taught how to do it. I wondered about Lucy Q. She was not on the swimming team, and her pale body in that loose bikini looked thoroughly inadequate for the task. Perhaps there would be another "incident." There would be a drowning and we must

Can I Sit With You Too?

return home and tell the benighted mother that her daughter was dead, too.

But something curious happened on that snorkeling trip, a delicate shift that had the impact of a proverbial epiphany. Lucy Q and I donned the mask and fins and spilled into the sea, kicking in the direction the native guide pointed. The waters were of bluer blues than had previously existed in my world, and the light flickered through them, dancing without rhythm.

There was entirely another world beneath those bluest waters. A parallel universe. A place of such great beauty that my mind reeled. I looked over and saw Lucy Q, her eyes magnified comically behind the mask. I could see she was smiling. The reef sprouted in strange colors and unlikely shapes that made me laugh and suck water into my snorkel, and the fish in their outlandishly loud costumes seemed unafraid of us, the clumsy observers. When we approached they spun around us with choreographed precision.

Lucy Q and I would raise our heads above the water to shout at one another about what we were seeing, and on one such occasion we saw our guide gesturing for us to swim into a cave with him. Once in the cave, he told us to swim to the back where we could dive underwater through a tunnel into another cave. It was pitch dark in the tunnel, he said. He would go first and pull us through by our hair. I felt my heart quicken, but both Lucy Q and I were so intoxicated by what we had seen that day that there was no turning back.

There was a blank moment of panic when I swam into nothingness and felt a hand grab my hair. My skull smashed on rock and I felt an urgent desire to turn back, but was pulled upwards suddenly into a glorious cathedral of rock and spectral light. And then Lucy Q surfaced beside me and I heard her shout, and it was a shout of amazement and triumph.

Looking later at Lucy Q's sunburned face and listening to her chatter on for the first time, I knew why my mother had brought her to this place. On this tiny island no one but us knew her misfortune. She had escaped her own context. She was here to understand that she was not inextricably tied to her tragedy, she had the rest of her own life at her disposal, and she had the option to fill it with adventure and elation.

Because of that trip, I learned early on the curative power of travel. And ever since I have lived with a reverent appreciation for it, knowing it permits us the incalculable freedom of perspective. And I like to think it was also a turning point for Lucy Q, who went on to do great things with her life.

Can I Sit With You Too?

Calling for Friends

~~~~~~~~~~~~~~~~~~~~~~

Kari Dahlen

Age twelve at the time

The summer before the seventh grade, I received an unexpected phone call.

"Kari! It's Trisha! You remember me, right?"

The voice was friendly but the name was not familiar. I probably uttered a noncommittal, "Um, hi!"

"You mean you don't remember me?" she asked, her voice a bit sharper. She didn't wait for an answer, "We were, like, best friends in the third grade." Her voice sweetened, "You remember—right?"

I refused to say, "yes." My best friend in the second grade had taught me not to lie. And in the third grade she told me music was from the Devil and as third graders we had to be "mature." Of course, we also had the Crazy Club in the third grade, and that wasn't particularly "mature," nor was being crazy particularly God-approved. But I didn't remember a Trisha in that mix.

I couldn't say "yes," but I also didn't want to admit not remembering her if she could be a potential friend.

That best friend from the second grade moved on to a Christian junior high while I went through several public junior high rites-of-passage such as having a seagull poop on my head during lunch, being accused of stuffing my bra, and having my locker broken into: the shelves my dad had built for me were doused with graffiti and the cheerful pink striped wrapping paper I used as wallpaper now had, "Kari is a Pig-Nose" written between the lines.

(The Pig-Nose thing was pretty unoriginal, but that didn't stop me from crying when a group of teenagers with their noses taped up high entered the frozen yogurt place where I worked a few years later. They specifically asked for me to serve their yogurt.)

In the sixth grade I ate lunch with a Chinese girl who wore her old school uniform, a shy Polish immigrant, a girl whose mullet stuck up in the front revealing heavy forehead acne, and a fickle, spacey girl who was repeating the seventh grade. Eventually, Mullet Girl decided she was too cool for me, so I stuck with the folks who didn't speak English.

If "Trisha" was real, maybe I would have a shot at a friend who was cooler than those others.

"Um, well, we must have been in different classes," I finally said to the voice on the phone.

"Nope!" Again, the voice was super-cheery and expectant. "Look, I am moving back into the area, and I wanted to see if you would show me around."

"Um, sure!" Finally I could answer in the affirmative. I could be bouncy, helpful, and friendly.

"Why don't you meet me on the steps on the first day of school?"

"Sure, absolutely!"

"You better remember me by then," she cautioned, and then laughed, "Bye!" Was that a giggle and snort I heard in the background?

I was skeptical and worried. If "Trisha" was pretty, she'd be snapped up by the "popular kids." And if she wasn't—well, then she'd be yet another person that I ate with because nobody else would.

The first day of seventh grade, I waited on the steps close to the location where eight months later I would overhear the football team telling their coach that if I made cheerleader they would all quit the team. I had made finals; they were panicking. I didn't make cheerleader.

I waited for Trisha.

And waited.

Perhaps there were giggles. Perhaps there were people hiding alongside a building, peeking out. But I didn't notice them.

After the second bell, I ran to class. Of course I was late, but I hadn't wanted to miss a potential friend. I didn't want her to think I stood her up.

That evening, she called again, "Um, sorry. I couldn't make it this morning."

I promised to wait for her again the next morning.

Of course, nobody came.

The call that evening was, "Where were you? I waited for you!"

I knew she hadn't arrived, had she?

I half-apologized, half-accused, "Well, sorry if you are real, but if you aren't, stop bugging me." I hung up without waiting for her response.

Fed up with public school life, I ended up at a private high school. But "Trisha" hadn't forgotten me the way I had apparently

Can I Sit With You Too?

forgotten her. That familiar voice phoned me shortly after my sixteenth birthday to inform me of a new dating service in the area. She didn't identify herself as "Trisha," but I am pretty sure it was the same person.

"No thanks, I have a boyfriend," I shrugged.

The shock in her voice was noticeable, "Well keep us in mind for when he dumps you!" I heard plenty of snickers in the background.

Two years later, the phone rang. "We are from the premier dance academy in the country. We saw your most recent performance and are interested in having you apply to our school. To where should we send the admissions materials?"

This was a joke, right? Still, I couldn't be sure, and I wanted to be polite, even if I had no intention of attending their school. I gave the voice my postal address.

A few minutes later, the phone rang again, "Oh, so sorry…" and then I heard a huge guffaw. The speaker composed herself and shushed her peanut gallery, "It turns out that you are not the dancer we are interested in. There are many better than you. Best of luck with your college applications."

"Actually, I've already been admitted to Brown University. But thanks for your kind wishes," I responded. I knew their call was a joke, but my statement wasn't a lie.

They called during the holiday break after my first semester of college to taunt me again with the fictional dating service. Fortunately, I was able to respond that their services were not necessary.

The next holiday break, the only calls were from my boyfriend.

I met a real Trisha years later. She is a gorgeous, thin, multi-talented woman. But she is also someone with a heart.

Mullet Girl is now quite beautiful and holds degrees in law and genetics. We are long-distance friends via holiday cards with occasional phone calls where I know the voice comes from a real person.

Christian Girl returned to the fold of our Crazy Club and we are now Crazy Mothers together.

A Giver

~~~~~~~~~~~~~~~~~~~~~~~~

Kat Kan

Age thirteen at the time

I was miserable when I started going to school in the United States.

Before then I had lived in Japan, as a military dependent with a Japanese mother and lots of family who accepted us mixed-race kids. Life was great.

Then we moved to Tacoma, Washington, where my father was stationed, and all of a sudden I became a pariah—for having a Japanese mother, for looking like the local kids with German ancestry even though I was mixed-race (how dare I!), and for getting good grades.

So, instead of trying to make friends, I closed in on myself. I turned to books and they became my friends; science fiction books and mystery books became particularly wonderful friends. Andre Norton became one of my favorite authors, and Mr. Spock on Star Trek was the character I most identified with. Simon and Garfunkel's song "I Am a Rock" was my anthem: "…and a rock feels no pain, and an island never cries."

When my father returned from a year's tour in Vietnam and we moved to Warner Robins, Georgia for my eighth grade year, I thought life might be a little better. The teachers seemed to like me, and the other students didn't really notice me, so I didn't get into trouble.

There was even one girl who said she wanted to be my friend, that we should exchange Christmas gifts. I bought her the best gift I could find for my one dollar monthly allowance (this was back in 1968), and I wrapped it and took it to school on the last day before Christmas break.

I gave my gift to her, and she thanked me and said she forgot my gift at home. She never did bring it by, not to my house, not to school. And now, thirty-nine years later, I can't remember her name.

It took me years before I would ever take a chance at making a friend again.

Un Angel Llamado Max

~~~~~~~~~~~~~~~~~~~~

Annelise Zoe Barriga

Currently in Seventh Grade

Translated by Sheryl Muñoz-Bergman and Liz Henry

Muchas veces me pregunto
¿Por qué te llaman especial?
A lo cual respuesta tengo,
porque eres angelical.

Many times I have asked myself
Why do they call you special?
The answer, I know,
Is because you are angelical.

Gran bendición Dios nos ha dado
al confiarnos a mi hermano.
Es una prueba muy dura
en este mundo ¡Mundano!

God granted us a great blessing
By trusting us with my brother.
It is a difficult task
In this mundane world.

Pobre de aquellas personas
que te ven como algo raro,
porque al verlas sólo pienso
en este mundo ¡Mundano!

I pity those
Who see you as odd,
They are limited by
This mundane world.

No conocen el amor,
ni el verdadero cariño,
ni el potencial de amar
de este angelical niño.

They do not love
Or know real affection,
Not even love's potential
In this angelical child.

Cuando dormir yo te veo,
yo me pongo a pensa
Que pasará por tu mente,
si sólo sabes amar?

Son tus sonrisas alegres,
son tus caricias tan tiernas.
Tu mirada es clara y pura,
tienes un amor sin límites,
¡Ay, hermano que hermosura!

¡La felicidad completa!
Yo la obtengo de mi hermano,
mi hermano especial
el que vino a este mundo
y nos enseñó a amar.

Voy a contar un poquito
de tu historia, hermano mío
porque tú desde chiquito
has destilado cariño.

Mis papás me han contado
de tu sufrimiento hermano.
Por todas esas operaciones
por las que has pasado.

Seeing you sleep
I ponder
What passes through your mind
If all you know is to love?

All your happy smiles,
Your gentle affection.
Unlimited love
In your eyes, clear and pure
My brother, such beauty!

Complete happiness
Is what I find in my brother
My special brother
Who came into this world
And taught us to love.

Here's a piece of your story
Brother of mine
Because since you were little
You've unleashed affection.

My parents have told me
Of all you have suffered
Through the many operations
That you have endured.

A pesar de todo eso
sorprendiste a los doctores
porque aquel niñito débil,
rompió todas sus predicciones.

Con tu aspecto frágil,
resististe a toda adversidad
y más que tristeza a mis padres
les enseñaste a conocer
la verdadera felicidad.

Me dicen que al nacer yo
tú aprendiste conmigo
y que compartimos siempre
un duro y arduo camino.

Cuando aprendí a gatear yo,
tú has gateado conmigo.
Cuando di mis primeros pasos,
tú los has dado conmigo.
Con mis primeras palabras,
hiciste el eco conmigo.

Recuerdo los hermosos y gratos
momentos
de nuestra añorada infancia,
en los cuales nuestros juegos
eran llenos de aventura y
fantasía.

Despite all these trials,
You've surprised even the doctors,
That a small weak child
could overcome so much.

With your fragility,
You resisted adversity
Instead of bringing sadness to
my parents
You taught them true happiness.

They say that when I was born
You learned along with me
And together we shared
A long and hard journey.

When I learned to crawl,
You crawled along with me.
When I took my first steps,
You joined at my side.
When I spoke my first words,
You were my echo.

I remember the wonderful
moments
Of our adored childhood,
When our games were full
Of adventure and fantasy.

Éramos los más grandes cómplices
al hacer e idear miles de travesuras,
pero recuerdo a mamá y a papá

reír y gozar al ver nuestras locuras.

Por años los dos compartimos
momentos felices y hermosos
pero también conocimos
momentos muy dolorosos.

Conocimos un grande dolor,
el tener enfermo a un padre.
El vivir el gran temor,
de poder perderlo por culpa del cáncer.
Pero recuerdo, ¡Oh Dios mío!,
ver tu fortaleza y fe.

Hasta hoy día te doy gracias
por todo lo que me enseñaste
que con inocencia y risas
ayudaste a sanar a nuestro padre.

Después los años pasaron
y a nuestra vida llegó
una hermanita querida
que a nuestra familia bendijo.

We were perfect partners
In mischief-making,
But I remember how Mama and Papa
Laughed and enjoyed our craziness.

For years, we two shared
Beautiful, happy moments
But we also knew
Very painful moments.

We knew the great pain
Of a father who was ill,
Living in fear
Of losing him to cancer.

But I remember, Oh My God!
Seeing your strength and your faith.

I remain grateful to you
For all that you have taught me
With your innocence and your smiles
You helped heal our father.

Then the years went on
And our family was blessed
With a dear little sister
Who came into our lives.

Al verte jugar con ella,
recuerdo los gratos momentos.
Tú continúas con juegos
que son recuerdos de mi
infancia bella.

Seeing you play with her
Pleasantly reminds me of times past,
As you play the same games
From my childhood memories.

¿Sabes hermanito amado?,
muchas veces he pensado
el querer ser como tú.
El aún conservar ese don hermoso
de poder ser cariñoso;
sin importarte siquiera
los problemas de afuera.

Beloved brother,
Often I have thought
That I want to be like you
To preserve the beautiful gift
Of unconditional love
Without ever worrying
About the problems of the world.

Por eso a este mundo reclamo,
a esta sociedad pregunto:
¿En donde se ha perdido la
inocencia de este mundo?
¿Por qué la gente no regala aún
más sonrisas sinceras?
¿En dónde quedó la verdad y el
amor a la hermandad?
¿Por qué ahora este mundo, es
un mundo material?

Thus, to this world I demand
Of this society I inquire:
Where has the innocence gone?

Why have heartfelt smiles been
lost?
Where lies Truth, and brotherly
love?
Why has this world become a
material world?

Oh, what sadness I feel
When I hear on the news
More wars,
And misuse of power.

¡Ay, qué tristeza me da,
escuchar en las noticias,
ver solo guerras y malicias
del poder en sociedad

Que ironía la de este mundo

llamarte a ti hermanito, ¡niño
discapacitado!

Cuando llegaste a esta vida

con la mejor habilidad,

¡la capacidad de amar!

Qué hermoso mundo sería,

si nos pusiéramos a imitar

el don que tienen los niños

llamados los "Especial."

Por eso orgullosa me siento

de tenerte como hermano,

de tener de hermano a un angel,

¡Un ángel llamado Max!

How ironic that this world

Calls you, little brother, disabled!

When you have come to this life

With the greatest of all abilities,

The ability to love!

What a beautiful world it would be

If we all were to imitate

The gift held by the children

Who are called "Special."

That is why I feel proud

To have you as my brother,

To have an angel as my brother,

An angel named Max!

Karen Morley

~~~~~~~~~~~~~~~~~~~~~~

Alison O'Brien

Age thirteen at the time

I hated Karen Morley in year eight. She had naturally blonde hair so light it was nearly white. Her no-makeup skin revealed colorless spots to the world. When she laughed her small teeth were yellow against the red of her too-large gums—and she laughed a lot. Her clothes were boring and old-fashioned, as if her gran had chosen them. She had no friends.

Despite all of that, the boys seemed to love her. They flocked around her like seagulls! She even had a boyfriend named Colin.

But she was so boring! She never said anything. She just laughed. She laughed at their jokes, she laughed when they teased her, she even laughed when they asked her questions, instead of giving an answer. But still they flocked.

Tania and I often stood nearby, frowning, arms folded, watching in disbelief. Now Tania and I—we were interesting, clever, and funny. We could joke back, tease them with attitude, and hold our own in any debate. We knew about football, politics, psychology, and Marc Bolan. We also spent a lot of time on our clothes, hair, and makeup. So why were they hanging around with her? She couldn't even crack a joke, and she had yellow teeth, for goodness sake!

I can't recall much about what we did to Karen Morley that year. I do remember Colin kicking Tania really hard for calling Karen names. I don't remember the names we called her, but I expect being boring and having yellow teeth were mentioned. We were outraged at Colin's reaction. We had just wanted the boys to see what we saw. They were supposed to turn against her, not us.

Three years later, Karen Morley and I sat together in the form room, just a couple of months from leaving school altogether. All animosities had long since ceased. We chatted and laughed about teenage girly stuff. Then suddenly she told me that Tania and I had made her life hell in year eight. She said we had sent her a card on her birthday, and when she'd opened it, "We hate you" was written inside. I was devastated for her. I saw all the pain of that year in her face.

Karen Morley was a nice, pretty, not particularly clever person. She had never done anything to hurt me, but I had really hurt her. I remember that I said I was sorry and did not know what else to say. I wish now that I'd told her what pretty hair she had, how attractive her laugh was, and how destructive and powerful jealousy can be.

Lines

~~~~~~~~~~~~~~~~~~~~

James Penha

Middle School

From the time he carefully
pulls the stool from beneath
the massive black slate
of the science laboratory table
    to align
    the outer edges
    of its rear legs
    perfectly
    against
    the line
    separating
    —looking
    backwards
    from the table
    —the black—the white
    imitation marble imitation marble
    tile tile
    from the white from the black
    imitation marble imitation marble
    tile tile
    on the left on the right
ahd arranges

the equipment required

for the experiment

to follow the set-up printed in the laboratory manual he stared at

so long last night at home

he fell asleep

before trying to revise his English homework

or reading consumer math,

Angel worries what he will do

forty-three minutes

and ten seconds from now

when Mr. Klepper

five minutes

before the bell

forty-two minutes

and fifty-five seconds from now

tells the class to clean up which means

Angel will be watched

forty-two minutes and forty-five seconds from now

to see if today he pushes the stool

back into the shadows

beneath the dark desk slab

where there is no line

to align

to its feet

so if Angel does push the chair

into chaos

his head will spin, stomach churn

and he will cough up what he didn't

in preparation for the day

eat for breakfast or

he will be given one last chance by Mr. Klepper

again to cooperate

before being sent to the office and

two hours

forty one minutes

and five seconds from now

detention instead of home,

so there is no time

or space to think of science

and he's falling

   per second per second

to earth

Miracle Turd

~~~~~~~~~~~~~~~~~~~~~

Lea Hernandez

Age fifteen at the time

"You turd!" I said.

The class was quiet because Ms. Hunt, least popular teacher in the school, had just walked in, and that was right when the word plopped out of my mouth and into the silence. Spoink.

The class gasped like they'd never heard that word before. The same class who snorted and smoked and got higher than the top tier of the Cotton Bowl, who used the f-word and the n-word as punctuation.

The same class who also called Ms. Hunt a word that rhymed with "bunt" but started with a "c."

Ms. Hunt snapped her look on me so fast that I thought I heard the sound of a whip crack. The detention for foul language came right after. Ms. Hunt didn't care that the reason why I called the boy in front of me a turd was because I came into English class from lunch and everyone already knew I'd wrecked a Drivers Ed. car before lunch.

I wrecked the car because Turd and the other two students in the back seat had been bagging on my driving, teasing me until I got so nervous that I bit the curb right at a storm drain and pinched the tire off the wheel. Instead of just the driver's ed teacher and Turd and the two other students in the car knowing, everybody knew. It was worse than going to a lunch of strawberry pie and stewed tomatoes after watching the Drivers Ed films of tattered flesh being pulled from mangled cars.

I got teased a lot in school because I was an easy, maladjusted target. I used big words, I'd say things that made no darn sense, say things meant to be funny or conversational that ended up creating silences like the one Ms. Hunt walked into. I didn't know how to own something as spectacular as wrecking a car. Instead, I went first-grade and said a first-grade word.

Ms. Hunt was by-the-book and a detention for saying "turd" was somewhere in the book; listening to me explain why I said it was not. Ms.

Hunt wasn't a bad English teacher; she was a good teacher who appeared to have no sense of humor and no heart.

The car wreck happened during football season, and was forgotten before Thanksgiving. Nine days before winter break, before Ms. Hunt came in for class, Turd stood up with an empty can and said, "Let's collect money to buy Ms. Hunt a tube of Preparation H for Christmas because she's such a pain in the ass!"

We laughed because it was a funny idea and it was true. Ms. Hunt was a pain in the ass. She deserved it.

Turd was daring, and would sometimes pass the can while Ms. Hunt stepped out of the room. We were about to die from glee by the day before our last day of school before break.

On the last day of English class before Christmas, Turd showed us the present. A nice big box, wrapped nicely and with a bow. Ms. Hunt came in, and the shiny faces and kindergarten-folded hands made her look at us suspiciously as she walked to her desk. We probably never looked that excited to see her before. Turd gave her the present.

"We collected money and got you something."

"Oh," Ms. Hunt said. It was the shortest word and sentence she'd say all year.

Ms. Hunt had a look on her face I'd never seen on her face before. I suddenly felt incredibly awful. The look on her face was like the one on my face when someone called my name and I thought this time it might be because I would be included, but knew I wouldn't be.

The gift was accepted. The Moment was here and the reality was that giving Ms. Hunt a tube of Preparation H wasn't funny. The idea was funny when the present was a can of change. Now it was a box being opened by someone who could be a grown-up me, who was about to experience a nuclear hurt.

The card was read.

The bow came off. The ribbon. The paper.

Ms. Hunt reached into the box.

Ms. Hunt pulled a bundle of tissue from the box.

I wanted so much to roll back ten days and tell Turd he was the pain in the ass.

I hated myself for not thinking of how I'd feel if I was Ms. Hunt. I was such a—turd.

The tissue fell away, and there was a mushroom-shaped canister. Nested inside of it were two more. A set of not-Preparation-H-oh-my-god-I'm-glad-I'm-alive mushroom-shaped canisters. Ms. Hunt arranged them in a row on her desk. Her eyes were red and shiny.

Can I Sit With You Too?

Of course, the canisters had been bought days ago, but they might as well have been a tube of Preparation H until the tissue came off. I can't say how this affected anyone else. All I know is the change was as fast as the moment between me cutting a pumpkin stem with a knife and cutting my thumb to the bone.

I had turned a corner, a razor-thin corner, and knew the difference between being an angry, thoughtless person, and being someone who thought about how what I did and said affected other people. I was redeemed. I didn't deserve it, but I was grateful for it.

Even if, especially because, I learned it from a Turd.

Double Standard

~~~~~~~~~~~~~~~~~~~~

E. Hansen

High School

Two students died in car accidents during my sophomore and junior years of high school.

The first one, Stewart, was a jock. He was a football team star, from an affluent family, and wasn't bad to look at either. My best friend had a crush on him.

One day he drove his dad's convertible to school, and then at lunch he and three friends went joyriding. Stewart rolled the car while doing fishtails on a dirt road, killing himself and putting two others in the hospital.

Before the day was out there were counselors visiting the classrooms, and a message over the intercom saying that overwrought students could be excused from class. We had a memorial assembly in the gym, and a poem was dedicated to Stewart during that year's graduation ceremony. A full yearbook page was devoted to him, and a memorial plaque still sits in the rose bed by the school library.

The next casualty was Alex, and he was not a jock. He dressed in black and hung out in the "pit" smoking with the "stoners." I respected him greatly. He was in my art classes, and produced work that could have sold in galleries.

One night while Alex was coming home from his part-time job, a drunk driver hit his car and killed him.

Alex's death was spread by word of mouth. No one was excused from class due to grief. His yearbook picture had a one-line caption that read "Alex **** (deceased)." The principal actively hushed any memorial efforts. One of Alex's friends was allowed to read a poem on the air in the cafeteria "radio room," but it was only heard by a few people.

There is no plaque for Alex; no one was allowed to speak about him at graduation. No one thought to use his death to start a "no drinking and driving" campaign.

Teachers teach that we should not be prejudiced towards others, but I saw first-hand just how prejudiced my school's administrators were: Let's honor the jock who killed himself being an idiot, and hide the death of the stoner killed by a drunk driver.

It Happened Several Years Ago...

~~~~~~~~~~~~~~~~~~~~~~

Jessica of BalancingEverything

High School

...but it's still something that brings tears to my eyes, and inspires me when I'm feeling low.

The public schools I attended from sixth to twelfth grade had amazing special education inclusion programs. Children with cerebral palsy, Down syndrome, autism, and other disabilities attended gym, biology, history, and other classes with their "typical" peers. As a result, I grew up with a fairly mature slice of the adolescent population. I never heard anyone with a disability get teased or made fun of. Popular girls and guys joked with the special ed kids in the halls, walked with them to and from class, and volunteered as aides in their homerooms.

I was very good friends with a girl named Vanessa who had Down syndrome. She made us a "Best Friends Forever" wallet card that I still have in my keepsake box. I was happy to see Jeff, another boy with Down syndrome, working at a local big box store a few years after we graduated. He would ride the bus and ask me if my friend Amy was willing to marry him yet.

Four years after I graduated from Murray High School, there were ten Homecoming Queen finalists. Two were girls with disabilities. Shellie Eyre had Down syndrome, and April Perschon had physical and mental disabilities due to a childhood brain hemorrhage. Since special education students usually stay for a few extra years, I knew Shellie from when I attended Murray High.

The finalists were escorted out to the gym floor by their fathers and dates. When Shellie and April walked out, the crowd rose to its feet, cheering and clapping.

Shellie's parents tried to prepare her for the possibility of not winning, but it was unnecessary. On that night, Murray High School crowned a beautiful girl with Down syndrome their 1998 Homecoming Queen. There wasn't a dry eye in the audience.

Kids can be cruel. The movies and media that show the popular kids regularly mocking and ostracizing the "losers" aren't that far off the mark. But stories like Shellie's do my soul good. Kids really can be mature, responsible, caring human beings. I'll never forget Shellie's face, beaming beneath her sparkly crown. April's too, because she was crowned an attendant.

Whenever I feel overwhelmed by all of the terrible things that happen in the world, I just open my old sheet of newspaper and read Shellie's and April's story again. And then hope in humanity makes everything feel better.

CONTRIBUTORS

~~~~~~~~~~~~~~~~~~~~~

Mike Adamick is a stay-at-home dad and writer in San Francisco. He loves to ride MUNI with his two-year-old daughter, Emmeline. Unfortunately, she likes to point at other passengers and say, "She has boobs like mommy," so he's afraid their public transportation days are numbered. Mike also likes cheese and blocks. His website is Cry It Out: Adventures of a Stay-at-Home Dad, at www.mikeadamick.com.

SJ Alexander lives in Seattle and was raised by a ferocious pack of wild badgers. In her spare time she enjoys hash runs, reading Victorian history, and hoping that someone will ask her kids to sit with them. She writes a few times a week at the website I, Asshole, www.iasshole.org.

Annelise Zoe Barriga lives in the San Francisco Bay Area. She is proud of her family's heritage and traditions. Her inspiration for writing this poem is her brother Max, who at birth was not expected to survive, but who has continued to defy all medical and academic expectations. Her family believes that Max has given them the great gift of true love, and that God gives special children to special families. This has made Annelise stronger and more prepared for the future. Some of her hobbies are drawing, writing, reading, and sports. One of her dreams is to go to Stanford University to become a doctor or veterinarian.

Dori Ben-David Johnston is a Kentucky native who moved to California for a "one-year adventure." Eleven years later she lives in the same house with her husband Andy, son Elliot, and daughter Jordan.

Louis E. Bourgeois teaches writing and philosophy at the University of Mississippi in Oxford. His prose poetics collection, The Animal, was released in May of 2008 by BlazeVox Books. Two more books, Colleen (VOX PRESS), and The Created Body (Xenos Books), are due out in 2009. Bourgeois is also editor of VOX PRESS. His web address is www.voxjournal.com.

Giedra Campbell lives with her husband and two daughters in Indianapolis. Beyond writing medical and technical documents for her day job, she annually writes the popular Campbell Family Christmas Letter. She could tell some good stories about one of the editors of this book, but is too polite to do so. Oh yes, and in her free time she writes stuff and cooks things.

Cheryl Caruolo holds a Master of Fine Arts in Creative Writing degree from Lesley University in Cambridge, MA. While her writing is diverse, she specializes in science, spirituality, memoir, and personal essay. Her website is www.wordforgebooks.com/authors.html.

N. Chandani is a full-time college student who enjoys writing about issues close to her heart. In her spare time she likes to spend time with her family and friends. Especially her inspiration JX!

Alison Chino writes about her days as the queen bee of the Chino House, a haven of life, love, and learning in North Little Rock, Arkansas. Her website is chinos.wordpress.com.

Lea Cuniberti-Duran emigrated from Italy in 1994, when she met her husband while vacationing in sunny Santa Cruz. She has lived in the San Francisco Bay Area ever since. Fourteen years later, she still hasn't learned how to surf, but can make a mean guacamole. When she is not busy chasing her three adorable but energetic boys, trying to catch up on sleep, or pondering on the meaning of "coco-nut," Lea runs her own graphic design studio, spends time with her handsome husband, and dreams of long vacations on tropical islands.

Kari Dahlen traded neuroscience research for some real-life subjects of her own, two boys whose mud excavations, craft projects, and fort-making keep her house messy but her heart full. She spends most of her time emptying her gas tank for the sake of gymnastics and soccer. Her personal website is The Karianna Spectrum: www.kariannaspectrum.com, and she also blogs at The Silicon Valley Moms Blog: www.svmoms.com.

Anna Dalprato has spent the last fifteen years traveling between Italy, where she lives, and the San Francisco Bay Area, where her three handsome grandchildren live. Anna enjoys spending months with them and watching them grow. Being far away from her beloved "Italia," often makes her homesick, although when in Italy she feels homesick for California. Anna no longer knits socks, and instead splits her time between quilting and being a news junkie.

Sarah Dopp has been writing, performing, publishing, building websites, exploring queer culture, and deviating from mainstream expectations since she was fourteen years old. You can see what she's up to now by checking out www.sarahdopp.com.

Because *Elisabeth Ellendorff*, daughter of a well-known German scientist, experienced a lot of moving as a child, as an adult she is quite happy to "belong" in the town of Bielefeld. Apart from being a teacher and an author, she is the mother of four lovely children, all of whom have grown up in one town and one country, as Elisabeth likes to stress.

Amy Freels lives near the Cuyahoga Valley with her loyal animal companions, Emma and Spaz. She enjoys designing books at all hours of the day and night. When she is not in her studio, you can find her outside, or remodeling her house. She enjoys poetry and is currently collecting letterpress type.

Brian Greene's short stories, personal essays, and writings on books and music have appeared in a variety of print and online publications, from 1991 to the present year. He was recently a semifinalist in the University of Iowa's annual book-length fiction contest. He was named the winner of the short fiction contest held by Jerry Jazz Musician in July of 2008. Brian lives in North Carolina with his wife Abby, their daughter Violet, and two cats.

Gwendomama was born in a small Pennsylvania town that is a bit of a suck-hole. She now lives in a small mountain community in central California, hopes to raise her children in the state without turning them into vacuous, self-centered egomaniacs, and would eventually like to retire to the tropical coast of anything.

E. Hansen still lives close to the Colorado city where she grew up. She is a happily married mother of one, and works as a teacher's aide in a nearby elementary school. She uses the experiences of her youth to help her better respond to her young charges. When not at school, she enjoys reading and crafts.

Liz Henry is a blogger, literary critic, poet, translator, and geek. She writes for BlogHer.org, othermag, Metroblogging, ALTA, Composite, and Feministsf.net; and has published poems, translations, and articles in Poetry Flash, Xantippe, Parthenon West, Strange Horizons, other, Two

Lines, Cipactli, Lodestar Quarterly, The Encyclopedia of Women in Science Fiction, and Literary Mama. Her site is www.bookmaniac.net.

Lea Hernandez is a twenty-plus years comics veteran who has published in traditional print and on the web. Her graphic novel series include Texas Steampunk, and the tart pop satire Rumble Girls. Her most recent work is "Ribbons Undone" for the Tori Amos (yes, THAT Tori Amos) Comic Book Tattoo anthology. Lea tried out for everything in school and still makes friends with the weird kids. She lives in San Antonio, Texas with her two special-needs kids and eight pets, only three of whom are cats.

Beatrice M. Hogg is a freelance writer who lives in Sacramento, California. She has an MFA in Creative Nonfiction from Antioch University Los Angeles. She facilitates a writing workshop at a local women's homeless shelter. Beatrice is working on several essay collections and a novel. Her essays have appeared in five anthologies and numerous magazines. She can be contacted at HoggPen57@yahoo.com.

Laura Eleanor Holloway is a resident of Bucks County, Pennsylvania, where she works as a graphic artist and has the great fortune to be part of a wonderful community of local poets.

Jessica of BalancingEverything is a mom to four who lives in potato country, where she runs a fabric business with her husband. She writes about her home schooling adventures at www.balancingeverything.com

Amanda Jones was born, raised, and educated in New Zealand, which means, like all New Zealanders, she has a hard time staying in one place for very long. She moved to the San Francisco Bay Area in her early twenties and promptly married an American. In order to have the ultimate cover for her peripatetic nature, she became a travel writer. She now writes for national travel magazines and newspapers. She does this in between raising her two proudly half-Kiwi daughters.

Kat Kan lives in the Florida Panhandle, where she works as a graphic novel selector for several companies, writes graphic novel reviews for several publishers, works part-time as a school librarian, has one adult son and one teenage son, and helps her pastor husband take care of their small, mixed-race congregation.

SK Knight is an artist, poet, and playwright who, after an earlier life in California, now lives in British Columbia, where she is renovating a 1910 farm house and chasing bears out of her orchard. Her paintings have been shown in California and Washington and her poetry has appeared on the web and in anthologies and books. Lately, she has taken up playwriting and has had some early success, with plays being produced in several states and a group show in New York City.

Suzanne LaFetra's writing has appeared in many magazines, newspapers, and literary journals. When she isn't feeding her chickens or racing to soccer practice, she's at work on a book about her love affair with Mexico. She lives in Berkeley with her two children and a prolific persimmon tree.

Victoria A. Laraneta is a grandmother of four who visits the small Midwestern town she grew up in every other year (on her way to yet another exciting USC football game). She loves living in the OC with her wonderful husband.

At the time this book was published, *lastcrazyhorn* was a second year music therapy graduate student attending Texas Woman's University. Her undergraduate degree is in instrumental music education. While student teaching, she discovered that the so-called "trouble" students were often the ones she worked best with. Then, in October 2007, she was diagnosed with Asperger's syndrome; a form of high-functioning autism characterized by difficulties with social skills. She now hopes to do music therapy with people on the autism spectrum after she obtains her master's degree. Her website is lastcrazyhorn.wordpress.com.

Amy Looper survived her youth to grow up and take a Web 1.0 Internet consulting firm public with several partners. Leveraging this little "golden egg" opportunity, she now is a dedicated social venture entrepreneur focused solely on building the next generation of web-based tools that help today's kids survive and navigate their world with confidence, one example of which is www.117media.wordpress.com.

Lisa Lucke is a writer living in the Sierra Nevada foothills with her shockingly handsome husband and four spotlessly clean children. Read all about her perfect existence at www.eatlanguage.blogspot.com

A. A. Matin was born in New York City and raised in Princeton, NJ. A graduate of U.C. Berkeley and member of Mensa International, he now lives in Santa Monica, California. Mr. Matin worked with former Vice President Al Gore on An Inconvenient Truth and has also been a part of such cinema classics as Halloween Resurrection. He also hopes his sister-in-law will convince his brother to move to L.A. so he can spend more time with his two beautiful nieces.

Madeline McEwen-Asker was born a Navy brat in Plymouth, England. She now lives in California. An Ex-pat from the UK, she is middle-aged, bifocaled, and technically challenged. She and her Significant Other currently enjoy fragile custody of three minors and a major, two girls, two boys, two with blue eyes, two with brown eyes, two with autism, two without. Her three websites are: alien-in-a-foreign-field.blogspot.com, whittereronautism.com, and sandwichedgenes.blogspot.com.

Pamela Merritt is the author of AngryBlackBitch.com, a staff writer for RHRealityCheck.com, and a contributing blogger to Feministing.com and Shakeville (shakespearessister.blogspot.com). Her writing has been published on Salon.com, in Salon.com's Broadsheet, and in the Chicago Sun-Times. Merritt is a featured commentator to NPR's Tell Me More with Michel Martin. She lives in St. Louis, Missouri with her two sorta-beagles Betsey and Theo.

Dan Moreau's work has appeared in Farfelu, Word Riot, and Segue. Other works are forthcoming in Lamplighter Review, Straylight, Faraway Journal, The Benefactor, and Twelve Stories.

After her short stint as a cool kid, *Katrina N. Mueller* became a pacifist, a doula, a comedian, a loyal member of Table 29, and a non-denominational nerd. She lives in the great state of Washington, although regrettably as far away from Seattle as one can get.

Jennifer Byde Myers grew up in Southern California, but moved to the Bay Area to try on Liberal; it felt good so she stayed and made a living writing and editing for large and small corporations. She loves playing in the woods, or anywhere, with her survivor-man husband and their two children, and has recently come to understand that there is no "normal" in her house. Jennifer chronicles her life as woman and wife while parenting both a "neurotypical" and a special needs child, at www.jennyalice.com.

Alison O'Brien lives by the river in a little town called Maldon, in England. She has had a chequered work history, including waitressing, teaching, secretarial work, and bar work in the UK, USA, Poland, Norway, and Spain. The most wonderful blessed part of her life is her thirteen-year-old son Scott, who never fails to make her laugh.

A native New Yorker, *James Penha* has lived in Indonesia for the past seventeen years. New Sins Press recently published *No Bones to Carry*, a volume of Penha's poetry, www.newsinspress.com/penha.htm. His award-winning 1992 chapbook, On the Back of the Dragon, is now downloadable at Frugal Fiction, www.frugalfiction.com/POETRY.html. Among the most recent of his many other published works are stories at East of the Web and Ignavia; and poems in THEMA and in the two Silver Boomers anthologies (Silver Boomer Press), Queer Collection (Fabulist Flash Publishing), and Only the Sea Keeps: Poetry of the Tsunami (Bayeux Press). Penha edits www.newversenews.com, a website for current-events poetry.

Ken Putnam lived his early years in Burnaby, British Columbia. He joined the Royal Canadian Mounted Police at twenty-two, and served for thirty-four years in Alberta, Northwest Territories, and Yukon. He is married with three sons, and now lives in Whitehorse, where he works as an investigator for the Yukon Department of Justice.

Wynn Putnam emigrated with her family from Holland to Ontario, Canada, in 1952. She moved to Vancouver, B.C., with her sisters in 1962. She enthusiastically embraces family, friends, fitness, film, books, and fun. Today Wynn and her husband Barry enjoy a vibrant city lifestyle in Vancouver's West End, where she frequently "talks and walks" around the seawall with her twin sister Betty.

Shannon Des Roches Rosa still thinks of herself as a socially-hamstrung introvert, even though she spoke in front of seven different audiences in 2008—including a speaker gig at BlogHer San Francisco. She usually lurks in her home office, writing about geography, children, parenting, autism, books, and how regular people should use complicated interfaces. She loves to stare into the limpid pools of her handsome husband's eyes, refuses to teach her spitfire daughters the word "demure," and adamantly brings her wonderful son (and his autism) to all the public places that make him happy.

Gerard Sarnat is a father of three and grandfather; physician, past CEO and Stanford professor; and virginal poet at the tender age of sixty-two. During the first half of 2008, he published or has work forthcoming in fifty-some journals domestically and internationally; in the second half, Gerry has been listed and won poetry contests/prizes within and outside the US. His first book, The Jonestown Homeless Chronicles, will be published by the California Institute of Arts and Letters' Pessoa Press.

Sabina Sood developed her passion for writing in the bustling Big Apple. She is now settled in Palo Alto, and keeps track of her busy life in a journal. In addition to writing, she enjoys playing soccer and oil painting.

Tina Szymczak lives in Windsor, Ontario. She is married to her soul mate, Adam and is the proud mother of two wonderfully spirited boys. Her life passions are her family, friends, and the inclusion of all people in all facets of society.

Mariann Vlacilek lives in Anaheim, California, with her husband Frank and canine daughter Bitsy. "Anaheim is very close to the coast, which is where I happily spent many of my formative years. My favorite place will always be near the ocean."

Wookie hails from Ontario, Canada, where she spends her days thinking up clever ways to hide her chocolate stash from her family, and trying to find science fiction novels anywhere in the county library system. During the day she is typically engaged in website development, client appeasement, and Tim Hortons acquisitions.

ACKNOWLEDGMENTS

~~~~~~~~~~~~~~~~~~~~~

How unbelievable that we managed to pull this all-volunteer effort off. Again.

We are indebted to the talented writers who let us publish their work on www.canisitwithyou.org and in this book. Thank you for having the courage to revisit these awkward times, and for sharing your stories with children who might otherwise think that no one understands them.

Thank you to Lea Hernandez, who sculpted, painted, composed, and photographed our cover art, *again*, and who came all the way from the Lone Star to the Golden State to let the audience at Book Passage see the woman behind the curtain—and the process behind her magical art.

Thank you to book designer Amy Freels, who once again volunteered to create our cover, and who did such an elegant job despite whirlwind deadlines and unanticipated hiccups.

Sincere thanks to SJ Alexander, for weaving us an introduction that demonstrates just how much she groks this project, as well as the kids behind—and in front of—these stories.

Thank you to our proofreaders Kristen Spina, Grace Mitchell, and Sheryl Muñoz-Bergman, who agreed to turn this much longer second manuscript around on such short notice, and who did such thorough and painstaking work. Thank you for the temporary loan of your brains, eagle eyes, and style manuals. Any remaining errors can be attributed to the sleep deprivation and adrenaline-fueled jitters of the editors.

Thank you to web professionals Craig Rosa and Liz Henry, who helped migrate the Can I Sit With You? website to its final, fully-enabled, ad-hosting home on Wordpress.org, thereby allowing us to shunt even more not-for-profit dollars from Can I Sit With You? to SEPTAR.

Thank you to all the people who hosted and helped us put together the numerous 2008's Can I Sit With You? shows, readings, and events: Cindy Emch of Queer Open Mic for putting together our show at Vince and Pete's Three Dollar Bill Cafe in San Francisco and donating the night's proceeds, Jason Kovacs and Bret Fetzer for arranging our show at Seattle's Annex Theatre, Chana Joffe-Walt from Seattle's KPLU/NPR, Peter Cuschieri of Angelica's Bistro in Redwood City, and Kate Ferguson and her events staff at Book Passage in Marin County, California.

Thank you to Marty and Janet Rosa for opening your cozy home to the Can I Sit With You? authors, and for throwing such a lovely party to celebrate our Annex Theatre show.

Thank you also to the Can I Sit With You? authors who performed at our events, and who read their very personal stories in front of live audiences: SJ Alexander, Michael Procopio, Liz Henry, Sarah Glover, Judy McCrary Koeppen, Cindy Emch, Jason Kovacs, Sarah Dopp, Jenifer Scharpen, Elaine Park, Lea Cuniberti-Duran, Jackie Davis-Martin, John Kim, and Amanda Jones.

Our sincere thanks to the friends and fans who attended our live shows, readings, and panels this year. Those shows live on, in the Photos, Videos, and Audio links on www.canisitwithyou.org.

Further thanks to the bloggers who promoted Can I Sit With You? on "teh internetz," Liz Ditz of I Speak of Dreams, Kristina Chew of AutismVox, Jennifer Graf Groneberg of Pinwheels, Amy Jussel of ShapingYouth, Mike Adamick of StrollerDerby, Kim Moldofsky of MOMformation, Carmen of Mom to the Screaming Masses, Brittney Gilbert of KPIX TV/cbs5.com, Cheryl Hagedorn of Blooking Central, and Laurie Toby Edison and Debbie Notkin of Body Impolitic. Special thanks to Susan Etlinger of The Family Room for wielding her impressive PR superpowers.

A final thank you to the people who provided much of the rocket fuel that kept this project going: Mona Springer and Bob Baldwin of Main Street Coffee Roasting Company, and Brent Goeway of Canyon Coffee Roastery. Thanks also for providing Can I Sit With You? with retail outlets.

Shannon wants to thank her husband Craig for supporting this project. She understands that sophomore efforts often lack the novelty of their predecessors—especially for those who get stuck with another round of solo-time riding herd on three wild and wooly children. I love you, and am so glad you didn't know my rather icky junior high self.

She wants her children to know that without them, this project would not exist. Gisela, Leo, and India, I know you'll always try to invite the quirky kids to sit with you. I hope these stories help to bubble-wrap your hearts during those times when my love is not enough to protect them. I am still pondering my position on adult involvement with playground bullies, but in the meantime please remember that your uncle Dave is an Army Ranger who loves you very much, too.

A heartfelt toast to her dynamic co-editor Jen for the positive energy that keeps this project going; for the talent, skills, and smarts that make our website and books possible; for having no fear about and propping up stage-frightened co-editors during speaking engagements; and for keeping the fridge stocked with beer and homemade treats. I feel very lucky to have your tall, blonde, and beautiful superpowers on my side; there would be no fabulous in my life without you.

A final thank you to her third-grade and all-time favorite teacher, Mrs. Gloria Radde, who read our first book, recognized so many stories that could have been her past and present students, and pronounced our project quite worthwhile.

Jennifer would like to thank her husband Shawn for his continued support in all things bookish and otherwise and for his ability to drive a Not-so-mini van filled with kids and moms and still look cool. Thank you for coming to every event, reading to the kids every night, and for keepin' on with me after ten years. There is no one with whom I'd rather road trip. You are the best choice I've ever made.

Thank you to my children: Jack, thank you for teaching me patience and always giving me something to write about; I am becoming the woman I want to be because of you. And thank you to my dear Kate for keeping me on my toes and constantly entertained with your antics; I can only imagine what a strong woman you will become someday, and I hope I can help you get there.

A sincere thank you to the amazing women I find in my life these days. I learn so much and feel so taken care of. You and your cat mugs make things like this possible when my life feels crazy.

And finally, special thanks to you Shannon, for your seemingly endless supply of energy, your desire to do the right thing allthetimealways, and for your magical meatball and sidecar making abilities. Knowing you has made me a better person, perhaps a little more tired, but better, certainly better, and smarter too.

Can I Sit With You?
www.canisitwithyou.org

www.ingramcontent.com/pod-product-compliance
Lightning Source LLC
Chambersburg PA
CBHW060348090426
42734CB00011B/2072